THE MAGIC OF ORDINARY

MELISSA GOUTY

To Mary,
One of the most
creative souls I know —
and one of the loveliest
people I've met.
Enjoy the read!
Missa

AMBER HOUSE BOOKS

CONTENTS

The Magic of Ordinary
by Melissa Gouty

A heart-tugging memoir of a daddy, his daughters, and the power of one good man to change the world...

Melford Johnson is an ordinary man. He has an ordinary job, lives in an ordinary southern Indiana suburb in the 1960's with his ordinary wife, and his three ordinary daughters. But Melford Johnson is also "Daddy," a man who can capture magic in the palm of his hand, sprinkle stardust over every occasion, and would pull down the moon for his three little girls if he could just so they could bask in its glow.

As seen through the adoring eyes of his daughter, Missi, Daddy takes the Johnson family on hilarious family adventures. But he also faces challenging situations with grace: delivering his own baby in a tiny bathroom in the middle of the night, winning over a suspicious mother-in-law, and discovering—at his own father's funeral—that he has a black aunt and an entire black family he never knew.

Missi pedals her bicycle with its banana seat and squirrel-tail streamer through an American landscape before cellphones, before social media, before cynicism. An America of swimming holes, wood-paneled station wagons, secret caves, Maw-Maws and Nannys, and hard won treasures stored away in piggy banks. An America where the greatest treasure of all is a father's love.

Whether Mel Johnson is the daddy you had or the daddy you only *wished* you had, you'll find yourself falling under his spell in a story that perfectly captures a time when innocence could still grow into optimism and love was all you needed to make magic and turn the ordinary into the extraordinary...

"Melissa Gouty writes the magical story of all our lives in *The Magic of Ordinary*. If you grew up in the 60's and 70's, this is an *Our Town* for our generation."—Teresa Medeiros, *New York Times* bestselling author

ISBN: 978-1-943505-79-1

Cover design by Control Freak Productions

Cover Photo © Molly Johnson

Published by Amber House Books, LLC

http://www.amberhousebooks.com

For more information, contact publisher@amberhousebooks.com

To fathers everywhere who light up their children's lives with the magic of ordinary...

Gratitude

Undying gratitude and love to my sisters, Melanie and Michele, who were unknowing accomplices to this book, who have their own "Daddy" stories, and who, alone in this world, shared these experiences. They understand the magnitude of joy in growing up with an ordinary man who made life magical.

For my daughters, Katie Elizabeth and Cassie Lauren, who made me see how much a parent could love her children and who make me wish every day that I could be more like "Daddy," bringing joy to their lives.

For my dear friend, Terri Medeiros who made this book possible in so many ways: encouraging my writing dreams for more the thirty years, publishing this book with Amber House Press, and opening her home and her heart to me in a lifelong friendship. To Martha Kay and Pam Johnson, my ardent supporters and beloved friends, who provided feedback on my manuscript and bolster me with emotional sustenance.

For my husband, Bill, who believes in me more than I believe in myself, who continues to work long past retirement so that I can write, and who loves me more than I can imagine.

EASTER 1963

"This is my Father's world,
and to my listening ears
all nature sings and round me rings
the music of the spheres..."

Hymn by Mark Schultz

DADDY MAGIC

"Look at that moon. Potato weather for sure."
—Thornton Wilder, *Our Town*

"Go stand on the back porch, Missi. RIGHT NOW! Be quiet. Don't say one word."

Daddy would never hurt me. Deep down I knew that. But still I was nervous. Not afraid, exactly, but tense and uncertain. Why was I worried about what Daddy was planning? But I couldn't stop the butterflies from darting around my belly when he commanded me, in no uncertain terms, to go stand outside in the dark.

"NOW! It has to be tonight," Daddy whispered as he pushed me out the door. "It's a full moon, Miss!"

My six-year-old-self nervously stood on the stoop, the tiny porch lit by moonbeams. A cool breeze rustled the leaves of the giant locust tree, and I shivered. When Daddy stepped out the back door into the moonlight flickering through the leaves, he looked like he was moving in slow motion. He came toward me, clutching something in his right hand. I nearly fell off the porch stepping backward, away from him.

"Don't move. Hear me? Stand still, Miss. This won't hurt. I promise. Just look at the moon and hold out your wrist."

Dutifully, I held out my arm, my eyes sliding down from the yellow moon to the face of this newly serious Daddy who, for once, was not laughing or singing.

"Now listen carefully, Miss. Look at the moon and take a deep breath."

I always did what he said and I looked skyward for a second before curiosity compelled me to look down.

Slowly, with his hand palm-down, Daddy crooned strange words and rubbed something hard and cold over my wrist.

"Abra-ca-da-bra. Ala-ka-zam.
  Moonlight and roses. This is our plan."

The words were linked together with a low warbling whistle from Daddy's puckered lips as he rubbed his magic talisman over and over my wrist in a circular motion.

The night sounds from the woods added a rhythmic accompaniment to the weird melody Daddy was creating. Goose bumps pimpled my arms and legs. Darkness and dappled moonlight disoriented me. For those few minutes, time stood still.

Daddy stopped mumbling and rubbing.

My mouth dropped open and I sucked in breath as I took in what he had in his hand.

"Daddy!" I squeaked in disbelief. "Is that a potato?"

A half of a wrinkly old potato. My dad had ceremoniously used half a wrinkly old potato to paint my wrist.

"But Daddy," I repeated, "why did you do that? What can one old potato do?"

"Just you wait and see," Daddy whispered. "We bury that potato and go inside. But don't you dare say a word about this to your mother or sisters. For the magic to work, it has to be a secret. Just watch. In a few days, your wart will fall off."

It did.

My dad was magic. All of his life, he conjured small enchantments and orchestrated minor miracles, just one of which was painless wart removal.

Everyone has a father. But I had a wart-whisperer, moon-musician, river-walker, cave-explorer, garden-guru, angel-hearing Daddy.

A man like any other. A man unlike any other.

Melford Henry Johnson was an ordinary man who—without trying—worked magic on those around him.

2
ANTI-MAGIC

"Every tooth in a man's head is more valuable than a diamond."
—Miguel de Cervantes

Screams came out of the garage. Horrible, gulping words... "You're killing me! I can't breathe! I can't breathe! "STOOOOOOOOO-P!"

My sister Melanie, at the time a cool teenager in my eyes, (she was, after all, thirteen), was laughing so hard she had to bend over and hold her sides to keep the laughter from breaking her apart. She wasn't alone in her merriment. Soon, we were both on the family room floor howling with laughter at the screeching coming through the garage door.

I like to think that being eight years old gave me an excuse to laugh at the misfortunes of others, especially my little sister. Years later, I know you shouldn't laugh at the pain of the people you love, but no matter how old you get, laughter can still erupt at the oddest moments. On this occasion, it happened because my younger sister, Michele, a feisty, curly-haired girl of six, was in the garage shrieking, "Daddy! STOP IT!!! You're KILL-LL-LL-ING ME!"

For days, Michele had complained about a loose tooth. She had touched it, wiggled it, and licked it with her tongue but could never quite muster the courage to pull it out.

I guess my parents got tired of hearing about the loose tooth, or they were just weary of waiting for that tenacious baby tooth to fall out. Maybe Daddy intended that this would be the magic moment he created for Michele—some tooth-extraction-special-spell he would perform for her like he did when he dissolved my wart with potato juice. Sadly, something went awry. Michele was neither calmed nor enchanted by Daddy's approach to tooth-pulling. She was livid.

Melanie and I were not privy to what Daddy intended when he went to pull Michele's tooth that Saturday afternoon. I don't know what Mother thought about all this, although it's important to note that Daddy decided to perform dental duty while Mother was shopping. Maybe he was going to yank that tooth out with his fingers. Quite possibly, he was going to implement what he so often joked about: tying one end of a string to the tooth and the other end to a doorknob, then slamming the door, causing the tooth to shoot out like a bullet. Maybe Daddy was just going to use his trusty pliers. But when Michele saw him coming at her, my little sister shrieked like a mating cat while her sisters rolled on the floor, laughing at her distress.

So much for sisterly love.

Melanie and I were so busy howling that we didn't even notice when the tooth came out or what Michele's reaction was. We did notice that she never again complained about a loose tooth or *any* kind of mouth problem. (Except maybe for the time she fell down the flood wall in old Clarksville on a field trip and got seven stitches in her upper lip.)

Whatever magic Daddy worked on Michele throughout

her lifetime, (and she has her own personal list of special Daddy-deeds) the tooth-pulling episode was definitely not one of them.

3

THE BUM'S CORNER

"I feel like our families were so interconnected, and we were so blessed to grow up in Blackiston Heights where our neighbors were our friends and our friends were our neighbors."
Letter from Janice McCreight Taylor to Michele, January 2015

"Guess what, girls?" Daddy asked as we stood on the front porch of our new house. "We now live on The Bum's Corner," Daddy declared as he spread his arms to take in the view. Our house, after all, was located at the intersection of Idlewood and Driftwood, both "idle" and "drift" being slow, aimless words. So Daddy named our spot in the new section of Blackiston Heights subdivision, "The Corner of Laziness and Sloth."

At the age of six, I had no idea what he meant, but I did remember going on an excursion with the Loebigs, close friends of Mother and Daddy. On one such Johnson-Loebig outing, Daddy and "Mr. Bill" got to laughing. "Mr. Bill" had a

7

loud, high, quick bark of a laugh. Daddy's was more of a headshake and chortle, but both grown men soon got going like a couple of teenage girls. They had read the names of two intersecting streets in a newly built subdivision. The signpost held two crossed signs bearing the words "Grinn" and "Berrit." Mr. Bill and Daddy slapped their knees, shook their heads, and wiped their eyes for what seemed like an hour.

Ever since that day, word nerd that I am, I have dreamed up street names that give a verbal tease when they intersect: "Rize" and "Shyne." "Upp" and "Atom." "Goforth" and "Conker." Funny what emotions a neighborhood street name can elicit. For the next fifty-eight years, the street name of Driftwood Drive—on "The Bum's Corner"—would evoke powerful feelings.

My earliest memories of our new house on Driftwood Drive involved four-year-old Michele and my six-year-old-self. We stood at the end of what seemed like a mile-long galley kitchen, brown cabinets on either side. (Space/distance perception changes as you age. I now know that the combined kitchen and eat-in dining area was probably only about twelve feet long.) My giggling sister and I created an utterly stupid game called "1-2-3, Fall Down!"

"ONE, TWO, THREE!" we'd shout in unison. On the count of three, we'd collapse in the craziest posture possible. Flailing our arms, squealing with laughter, faces contorting, we whoomphed and thudded and landed on the shining new linoleum. The "1-2-3, Fall Down!" game had no rules, rhyme, or reason. It was created spontaneously, without thought, like the beginning of a rain shower or the appearance of a cloud. Its only purpose was to amuse each other, and in that, we thoroughly succeeded. Giggles overcame us every time we fell to the floor, far more important than the minor bumps and bruises we'd find the next day.

Little did I know the role that kitchen would play in memory. In the narrow corridor between the cabinets, we cooked meals, did dishes, played games, ironed clothes, spent thousands of hours eating around the brown table, and learned to dance. In that small bit of floor space, Daddy would teach all three daughters to dance by putting our feet on top of his, counting out loud, and stepping out a pattern. The older we got, the less we needed the guidance of Daddy's instep. By junior high, any one of the three Johnson girls could follow his lead in both the jitterbug and box-step.

Childhood games and dancing with Daddy were not the only clear memories of those early days in 1964 in our new house on Driftwood Drive. Another one comes through the fog of age clearly. I got a severe chiding from Mother for repeating things I heard at home. Apparently, I made a brash statement to the driver of our "Jack and Jill" kindergarten van. When she asked how the new house was coming along, I put my hands on my hips and shook my head, mimicking an exasperated adult. "All it does is cost money, money, money!" I spouted, quoting Mother and Daddy's overheard conversation.

Ours was not a fancy house. But the sturdy, mid-sized ranch house with its three bedrooms and one and a half baths was my parents' dream home, built on a corner lot in a new subdivision in the growing community of Clarksville, Indiana. Kids who lived there in the sixties and seventies led a halcyon existence, even if we didn't know it at the time.

We held square ball games in the middle of the street, sketching chalk squares on the road directly center of the Heldman's front yard. On our street, boys far outnumbered the girls, which probably made Driftwood Drive more rambunctious and more competitive than if the mix had been the other way. The three Pope boys lived next door to us. The three Heldman boys lived across the street. At any given time during a summer day or evening, kids from the two-parallel-streets, Driftwood and Briarwood, would be found bouncing that red ball from square to square in fierce but friendly 4-square competition.

Kickball was another favorite. No matter what game we played, the sewer/water plate in the middle of the street was always home plate. A black street number painted onto the curb in front of the Heldman's house was first base. Second base was always a moveable item like a smashed box or an old rag since we had to pick it up and run to the side of the road when cars came. Third base was the black metal Johnson mailbox. Many a game was played by Greg Heldman, Steve and Chris Pope, my sister and me. Sometimes we'd have a bigger game when the kids from Briarwood cut through their backyards to join us.

The Briarwood kids, the Hammans and McCreights, lived across the street and through the Heldman's back yard. Between these two families, there were eight kids, including Michele's best friend, Janice McCreight, lovingly called "Janny." Blackiston Heights families had kids in the same age range, attending the same schools, experiencing similar hard-working, middle-class, ordinary Midwestern experiences. We were neighborhood families connected by proximity and mutual morals.

Interconnected.

Jackie Hamman was the oldest of the Hamman kids. She was a year or two older than Melanie and was an excellent, often-available, babysitter. Both my parents worked, so for several years when Melanie was off working as a camp leader at the Parks and Recreation Department, or when she was attending daily cheerleading practice, Jackie took care of Michele and me since both our parents were gone during the day. Our favorite babysitter, Jackie was tall and slender, with a pale complexion and big, blinking eyes that always reminded me of Bambi. It was Jackie who was babysitting the evening I went sauntering around in the yard barefoot.

"Owwwwww!" A scream of shock and pain reverberated down the street. "OOOOOOOwwwwww! It b...b...urns!" I hopped up and down on one foot, dangling a giant yellow-jacket from the other foot until Jackie came swooping down from the front porch like a mama hawk picking up its chick. She swept me into her arms, carried me inside, and deposited me on my stomach on the couch in the living room. Carefully, gently, she removed the black and yellow striped bee from the crease on the bottom side of my big toe, crooning all the time, "You'll be okay. You'll be okay."

Jackie did her best, but no babysitter—no matter how competent—can fight bee allergies. In no time at all, huge, thick, itchy red hives erupted all up and down my legs. Soon they covered my entire body, swelling in the space between my thighs and torso, behind my knees, and all over my belly. My body looked like some weird, puffy, red-spotted leopard. I can still see Jackie's big eyes and pale face as she carefully set me in a bathtub filled with warm water and baking soda, ever so gently rubbing my splotchy body until Mother and Daddy got home.

That night of the bee sting, Jackie proved her worth as both medic and psychiatrist, calming and soothing my body and soul. That night was the first time I'd ever gone barefoot, the first time I'd ever been stung, and the first time I knew I had a bee venom allergy. A few days later my big toe, still swollen, red, and painful, had to be lanced.

Jackie was a great babysitter, even though one other night she nearly killed us by scaring us to death.

Michele and I had just watched a frightening episode of *Lost in Space*, our favorite show. I wanted to go on a space adventure and be pretty, perky Penny Robinson with a long, dark ponytail. She, after all, didn't have my head of ugly, mangy, coarse hair. At the same time that I wanted to be Penny, I knew that I was in love with smart, freckle-faced, resourceful Will Robinson. (At the age of seven, I didn't understand the potential dilemma of wanting to be a sister in love with her own brother.) The episode Michele and I had just viewed involved the detestable actions of Dr. Smith and a horrifying, outer-space creature. (Didn't they all?) We went to bed right after the show, obediently following the bedtime rules dispatched by Jackie. Still a little scared by the alien monsters, we snuggled under our blue chenille bedspreads and were just drifting off to sleep when the bedroom door swung open.

A faceless, unrecognizable shape staggered toward our beds, waving its arms in threatening gestures. I saw the monster first, silhouetted against the light from the hallway. My shrieks alerted Michele to danger. She chimed in, both of us screaming at the top of our lungs, both of us standing up in our beds, backing up to the wall, trying to put distance between us and the attacking "thing." The noise of our own squealing was the only thing I could hear, but the rest of the neighborhood heard those silly little Johnson girls bellowing that night.

"Oh, girls! Stop! Please be QUIET!" Jackie pleaded as she shed the parka she had put on backwards over her arms and face. It was a simple trick, but to us she had been a master of disguise, expertly impersonating an extraterrestrial monster by kneeling down and walking into the bedroom on her knees, waving her arms wildly, oblivious to the terror she would create.

"Look! See! It was just me with my jacket on over my face," she explained as she tried to calm us. Her eyes were almost as wide as ours, but only with fear for what she had done to us. "Don't worry. I promise. Nobody's here. Nothing will hurt you!" Jackie's soft voice trembled just a bit. "I was just playing a joke on you. There are no monsters! I didn't know you'd be so scared."

Watching *Lost in Space* as a grade-schooler was totally different than watching it as a high-schooler. The creature we thought was terrifying was fake and funny to Jackie. Big kids just weren't afraid of anything.

Jackie calmed us down by reading stories out loud. We got an extra half-hour before we had to go back to bed and an additional snack was involved to placate us. Being screaming sissies had its own rewards.

Other than a great scare, nothing beat a summer night in the neighborhood.

Hide and seek games were frequent and frenzied. Kids flew out from behind bushes and huddled behind garbage cans. We spread out through the yards and porches of the two different streets, straining to hear "You're It!" while dancing with the lightning bugs until Dickie Pope's shrill whistle signaled all of us that it was time to come home. We looked for four-leaf clovers, made rubber band jump ropes, and folded gum-wrapper chains. We played clapping games with our hands.

> *"My boyfriend's name is Lucky.*
> *He came from old Kentucky*
> *With rings on his fingers and bells on his toes.*
> *That's the way my story goes.*
> *He gave me all his peaches.*
> *He gave me all his pears.*
> *He gave me all his fifty cents and*
> *Carried me up the stairs."*

(Hmm… Is this a jingle about paying for feminine favors? And Mother actually let us sing it?) And, ah, the jump rope! Long ropes turned by neighborhood kid twirlers on either end: "R-E-D-H-O-T, red hot, red hot, YESSIREE!" Such simple pursuits in a time before computers and cell phones. Before parents worried about child abductions, sexual perverts living next door, and drug dealers lurking in the dark.

And oh, the theatrics!

One of our favorite pastimes was producing plays and talent shows on the McCreight's back patio. Michele and Janny commandeered the effort, but I was usually included, along with anyone else who could be coerced onto the stage. A couple of times every summer, we would plan an event and give every kid some role in the production. It might be singing. It might be performing a skit. It might be a newly choreographed dance. Costumes and props were required, and we'd raid our homes for jewelry, clothing, bed sheets, construction paper, glitter, glue, and whatever decorations were handy.

Even Mother, often aloof and more comfortable hibernating in the house, would come to the latest neighborhood show. Our parents hauled lawn chairs over to the neighbor's backyard and the other parents joined in to watch their children play-act some silly skits and mouth some banal music. (It's not like any one of the Blackiston Heights kids was a musical genius or theatrical protegee.) We were just kids entertaining ourselves and having fun. The friendships forged by the kids through these performances forged friendships for the adults as well.

Mitzi Hamman and Barb McCreight, both stay-at-home moms of four children each, were good to us. They would pile their kids, the Johnson girls, and any of the neighborhood boys who wanted to go into the blue station wagon for an outing to Deam Lake. All day long we'd splash and play in the water, run in the sun, and eat peanut butter sandwiches on white bread out of a cooler. (Only as an adult did I realize the inherent kindness of these women who willingly took responsibility for children who weren't their own. I am not up to the gargantuan task, but they did it frequently, effortlessly, and with tremendous joy.)

While producing plays was fun and swimming on a hot summer day was exciting, those activities were not nearly as long-lasting as the years we spent riding bicycles around Blackiston Heights, one of the few things we did that required actual equipment. It was Daddy who made sure that Michele and I could be part of the crowd.

"Go straight to your room. Do not come out. And I mean it!" Daddy barked one Christmas morning.

We had no doubt that he did mean it. Neither Michele nor I had ever heard Daddy use that stern tone, and certainly never on Christmas morning. We were almost scared, but we knew we hadn't misbehaved. Giggling nervously, we ran down the hall to our bedroom and slammed the door. There we hovered like manic moths darting to and fro, listening for Daddy, exchanging anxious glances, covering our mouths, and hopping from one foot to another.

"Okay, girls. You can come out now, but you've got to close your eyes and hold hands. Go slow. And *don't* open your eyes!" Daddy's voice boomed from outside our bedroom door.

Too scared to disobey, we clutched each other's fingers and walked blindly to the living room.

If Michele and I had an inkling of what lay before us, I don't think we would have felt the intense joy that walloped us when we saw two metallic-colored Stingray bicycles sitting in front of the Christmas tree. Those bikes were a total surprise and "The stuff that dreams are made of," at least to two young girls. Michele's bike was green. Mine was blue. Both came with white wicker baskets trimmed with pink roses.

Daddy smiled. "I picked them for you to match your eyes."

Those Schwinn Stingray bikes were our ticket to adventure. Nothing else was quite like careening around the neighborhood on my blue bike. For years, I rode up and down driveways, as fast as possible around the block, over the curbs and around the street drains that framed Driftwood Drive. Freedom was propelling myself forward, feeling the breeze on my sweaty skin, seeing the rest of the world whizzing past me in a burst of speed, feeling like nothing in the world could hold me back.

Our bicycles became truly extraordinary when Daddy gave us a taste of his own childhood to embellish our two-wheelers as we rode around Blackiston Heights.

Daddy was a country boy who loved hiking, camping, swimming, fishing, and hunting. Every once in a great while, he would get the urge to go squirrel hunting like he did when he was a kid. Whenever he did, we would dine on squirrel meat, gravy, and biscuits. We ate squirrel when Daddy hunted, not because we needed the food, but because he wanted to use what he had killed. While I didn't particularly like squirrel, (it was hard to eat without getting a bite of buckshot,) I wasn't appalled at the idea, either. Instead, I thought it was really "cool" that Daddy was doing what the pioneers did—shooting something and bringing home a different kind of dinner than hamburger or chicken. How many kids in the neighborhood could say they were having "frontier food" for supper?

And how many kids would end up sporting fluffy, red squirrel tails on their brand new bicycles?

"Please, please, please, Daddy," Michele and I whined in unison as we stood in door of the open garage watching Daddy clean those squirrels. "Please, Daddy? Can we have them?"

For weeks after that hunting trip, my sister and I would pedal around the neighborhood as proud of ourselves as if we were driving a Mercedes. The squirrel tails flapped behind us, hanging off the handlebars and back fenders of our powerful, new Stingray bikes. We thought we were hot stuff.

Today, animal rights groups might be horrified, but apparently nobody in Blackiston Heights reported us for squirrel-skinning. Our neighbors might have wondered about those strange little Johnson girls as they pedaled furiously on their banana-seated Stingrays with decaying rodent tails flying behind us. But our neighbors, who were also our friends, embraced our quirkiness, smiled at our foibles, and dismissed our addiction to fur.

But the neighbors didn't know about a different addiction. I was an addict. A Coke addict. Not "Coke" as in cocaine, but Coca-Cola. My childhood home was where I learned about cravings and insatiable thirsts. Longing and lust for Coke. At night, Mother and Daddy would knowingly torture me. The house would be quiet after we were put to bed. Then slow footsteps in the kitchen. The creak of the kitchen closet door. The roll of the silverware drawer. Suddenly, cruelly, I would hear that distinctive "PHFZZZZZZ" and the clank of a metal bottle cap falling onto the kitchen counter. That unique sound traveled down the hallway and through the closed door of our bedroom, making me salivate. I was so thirsty! A wicked sweet tooth and the abject denial of something I wanted so badly caused me to make a vow: "When I'm grown-up, I will have as many Cokes as I want, whenever I want, wherever I want."

I was insanely jealous when Melanie, being the older sister and a teenager, received a six pack of bottled Coke (the very best kind) as a Christmas gift. I made sure to not misbehave if Mother and Daddy went out for the evening and told a babysitter, "If they're good, they can have a Coke and some popcorn…" Remember Jiffy Pop before the days of microwaves? "Jiffy Pop, Jiffy Pop, the magic treat. As much fun to make as it is to eat." There was no way I'd do anything to jeopardize our Friday night Coke and Popcorn Fest while watching Star Trek, boldly going where no one else had gone before.

Kids. Games. Bikes. Cruising. There must have been times when friends fought and tempers flared. There must have been some hurt feelings, snubbed noses, and stubbed toes over the years, but I don't remember those. Only the good memories survive.

One of my favorite recollections happened on an early morning in April 1976, the year I graduated from high school. It was warm and sunny, and Ted Hamman drove their blue station wagon to school with Janny McCreight, Michele, and me as passengers. We were a carpool of straight-arrow, smart, happy, polite kids who lived less than a hundred yards from each other. As I had every day of that year, I sat in the front passenger seat, my lap piled with massive textbooks and my voluminous purse slung over my shoulder.

The other kids must have been planning this for days. I never knew if it was a joke on me as a near-graduation-era senior or because I was the most naïve and most oblivious person in the car.

When Ted pulled up to a stop sign, the car doors flew open, and all three of the other people in the car started running around the car yelling and shouting, "Chinese Fire Drill! Chinese Fire Drill!" I sat paralyzed on the front seat, weighed down by twenty-five pounds of textbooks and a brick wall of bewilderment. By the time I picked up my books, balanced them in my arms, tugged the door handle, and disembarked to run the required laps, I was laughing hysterically. I stumbled by the front wheel, nearly falling off my cork-bottomed platform shoes. I finished running around the car by myself like a chicken with its head cut off. Everyone else was already back in their seats, delightedly watching their spastic friend.

At Mother's funeral visitation, Ted Hamman, who I hadn't seen in four decades, asked me, "Do you think we had such a great childhood because of the era we grew up in, or because of the neighborhood itself? Was it that section of Blackiston Heights that held its own kind of special magic? Or was it just the luck of the draw that the right people came together at the right time?"

All of the above. It was the era. It was the neighborhood. It was the kids and the families and the very smell of the air in a simpler time in a different decade. Mostly, it was because we were blessed with good, kind, hard-working parents who loved us—regular people who created an aura of protection and playfulness around their kids.

But it was "Daddy" especially, an average guy with an amazing capacity for happiness, who made magic out of ordinary and life out of love.

December 1962

4

SWIMMING AT THE YMCA

*"It's been another rainy day, at least until three o'clock. I went
swimming about five o'clock. The water is wonderful, and I
certainly enjoyed the swim. They have a few "NO SWIMMING"
signs up, but so far, so good."*
—Letter to Molly, May 24, 1952

The story always ended with his hands thrown up in the
air and a whoop of uncontained laughter. His tale
never lost its power to entertain even after years of telling.

"Well, you know, I enlisted in the Navy. I wanted to be a
gunner, but was stationed in Philadelphia as a clerk after I
graduated, I guess because I could type. I didn't have much
money, and back then, the YMCA's offered inexpensive
rooms for servicemen. So that's where I lived." Daddy lifted
his shoulders in a "no-big-deal" gesture.

How much his typing ability did to place him stateside as
a clerk at the end of WWII I don't know, but he always
impressed upon his daughters that everybody should know

how to type, both men and women. Before the war, many men took typing classes since women weren't yet a major part of the workforce. The ability to type was a skill that enhanced his entire life. Many are the typewritten letters and cards mailed out from that old black mailbox on Driftwood Drive, missives that crystallize his very essence in simple carbon keystrokes.

Daddy didn't place undue demands on his daughters, but one of his life rules was that we master three skills: typing, swimming, and driving. He didn't want us to be weak women who had to be taken care of by husbands. In his mind, it was a simple formula: typing provides employment; swimming gives joy; driving offers independence. Of the three skills, swimming was, by far, his favorite.

"The Y was perfect for me!" Daddy would crow. "Other service men lived there, so I wasn't alone. It was walking distance to headquarters, and it had a full-sized pool for swimming—which I loved. I could come home every day and just take a dip in the pool."

Being the river rat that he was, swimming was as natural and relaxing to Daddy as it was for an otter.

"You know, back then, we all swam naked." Daddy looked around, purposely trying to shock us.

No way. We all knew he skinny-dipped in the river or the rock quarry, but surely Daddy didn't mean that he swam nude in public?

"Yep. Buck naked. Not a stitch of clothing. It was really kind of nice. You didn't have to worry about anything," Daddy threw up his hands in an "abandon-all-caution-throw-your-cares-to-the-wind" gesture. "Believe it or not, you weren't ALLOWED to wear bathing suits, and I was glad."

"M-E-L!" Mother growled. "You don't have to go into detail." The very mention of the word "naked" made Mother go into tight-lipped, stiff-necked, rigor-mortis-of-the-mouth.

Since his friends from camping and rafting adventures frequently mentioned his strong propensity for skinny-dipping (even at his funeral), I can rest assured Daddy had no qualms whatsoever about wearing his birthday suit to public places.

The story wasn't over yet. Daddy's voice dragged me from watching Mother clench her jaw back to watching his animated face.

"Well, as usual, one night I went out for my nightly swim. I opened the door and walked right out to the edge of the pool. Just before I dove in, I looked up to see a woman sitting on a bench. Her arms were flailing in the air above her head, her mouth formed a giant "O", and she was screaming at the top of her lungs."

Daddy's arms whacked at the air above him as he mimicked the woman. "It's a sight I've never forgotten. The site of that lady yelling and flapping like she'd been shot!"

"Ha!" His laugh was loud and contagious. "You see, girls. You're not allowed to swim naked on FAMILY night!"

Years later, I learned that pools of the past didn't have good filtration systems. Because old-time swimsuits had a lot of wool fiber that clogged the filters, the thinking was that swimming in the buff was best. In fact, The American Public Health Association mandated nude swimming for men from 1926 until 1962. Coaches and pool managers would do full body inspections to make sure that there were no open wounds or diseases going into the pool.

Full body inspections. Are you kidding?

Daddy didn't mind. He didn't care who looked. He just wanted to swim.

But he did learn to check the schedule for Family Night at the Philadelphia YMCA.

5

TIGHT-ROPE WALKING

"Your Mother called just a few minutes ago. She wanted to know what my name was. She said she had told the man who was going to print the announcements that my name was Melton. It's a good thing she called or I may have had to change my name to correspond with the announcements. Couldn't have you marrying the wrong guy. I couldn't help but laugh. I told her my first and middle name was Melford Henry and that my last name was Johnson."
—May 20, 1952 letter to Molly

Her dark dress with polka dots and a lace collar was the epitome of style in 1952. A double strand of pearls ran properly under the collar, and on her left shoulder, in just the perfect spot, was a corsage. Her strawberry blonde hair was drawn back into a svelte chignon. Her arms were crossed in a smug "I-told-you-so" attitude. Her teeth were bared in what passed for a smile.

The wedding photographer snapped this casual shot of a

23

new mother-in-law talking to her new son-in-law. The picture appeared totally innocuous and found its way into my parents' wedding album with black and white photos from that special day, July 11, 1952. Long after that photo was taken, Daddy explained, with just a hint of rancor, what was really going on. The grandmother we called "Nanny" had just delivered a forked-tongued remark with the speed of a striking snake. While he would recover, using humor as an anecdote to her venom, the wound Iona inflicted would stay with Mel the rest of his life.

"Well, well. Now that you've got her, you can divorce her in a few months."

Iona Wilson's words were delivered in a conversational tone. No one around would have ever known the unkind thing she had just said to because she disguised the sneer in her voice with the "smile" on her face.

What had the young Mel Johnson done to deserve such an insult?

Mel Johnson had never been in any trouble. He had served in the war, gone to college on the GI bill, landed a decent job, and built a house. He had a close family who loved him, had lived in the area his entire lifetime, and wasn't a drinker, a gambler, or a rebel. So why was Nanny so unkind?

Iona Wilson must have been worried about the same thing that bewildered the rest of us for years. How could two people as different as my mom and dad make a life together?

Mel was a country kid who relished the rugged outdoors. Molly was a pale-faced, sheltered, indoorsy girl who enjoyed books and poetry. Mel had served in the Navy and had seen a bit of the world. Molly had never left the state of Indiana. Mel was gregarious and charming. Molly was timid and aloof.

Nanny probably knew that while opposites attract, they don't always co-exist.

It was impossible for a woman like Iona Wilson to keep her opinions to herself, so she uttered the now infamous words: "Well, well. Now that you've got her, you can divorce her in a few months."

Nanny's comment stung like a hard slap in the face. Surprised by her contempt, Daddy shook it off and laughed, "Well, Iona. Congratulations to you, too," before moving off to greet another wedding guest. Daddy may have been taken aback by Nanny's remark, but this wouldn't be the first—or the only—time he would glimpse Nanny's dark side. It certainly wasn't the auspicious beginning of the marriage that he had hoped for.

He was playing tennis when he met my mom in the summer of 1951. She was watching the action on the courts with some girlfriends when something unexplained happened. A vibration from a thwacked tennis ball. A bead of sweat that flung a pheromone of attraction toward Mother. A close-lipped smile that slipped off my Mother's face and into Daddy's heart. Who can know the forces that draw people like magnets to each other?

Mel and Molly started serious dating and correspondence in January of 1952 after a winter dance. Daddy wrote to Mother daily for the six months she was at Indiana University before the wedding.

In anticipation of gaining a daughter, Daddy's parents, Henry and Marguerite Johnson, invited Molly's parents, J.C. and Iona Wilson to dinner, took them strawberries, and extended the hand of friendship in gracious, open-palm gestures. Daddy took Bill, Mother's younger brother, fishing. Daddy's courtship with my mother was through correspondence, and then by dating her on weekends when she came home from Indiana University, and then transporting her back to campus on Sunday afternoons. He often drove up to Bloomington to bring her home to New Albany for the weekend before taking her back to school on Sunday afternoon.

Mel Johnson asked Molly Ann Wilson to be his wife, and their engagement was announced on April 11th, 1952. A church wedding was planned three months later. My sister, Melanie, was born in September of 1953, one year and two months after the wedding.

Daddy had done nothing to cause such vitriol from his future mother-in-law.

Nanny, however, wasn't about to let the wedding happen without making her presence known. After Daddy and Mother announced their engagement, Nanny had the gall to telephone Daddy—get this—to find out his name. Hmm…. Can you imagine how that conversation went?

- **Iona to Mel:** *I'm calling you because even after months of dating, declaring your intentions, and giving my daughter a ring, I don't remember your name. Who are you, really?*
- **Mel:** *Hello to you, too, Iona.*
- **Iona:** *So the man is getting ready to print the announcements. I told him your name was Melton, right?*
- **Mel:** *Now, Iona. You know my name. My first and middle name is Melford Henry. My last name is Johnson."*

If it were me having this conversation with my future mother-in-law, I would be gritting my teeth, spitting, sputtering, and preparing for verbal battle. Daddy, however, declared, "I couldn't help but laugh." Being able to laugh at the absurd was one of his greatest gifts.

In the years that followed, like any good husband, Daddy worked to become part of mother's family, attending all the Wilson family gatherings, laughing and smiling as always. He was especially simpatico with Aunt Bonnie, another "outlaw," the wife of mother's brother, Bill. Through the next four decades, Daddy and Aunt Bonnie would exchange funny cards, sharing a sense of humor, the ability to laugh, and a vague sense of "otherness." Daddy eventually made his peace with Nanny, which was like walking a tightrope over the Grand Canyon.

Nanny eventually got over her huff about her daughter marrying a man named Melford Henry Johnson. Like everyone who ever met him, Iona grew to love him. As the decades rolled on, she came to rely on Daddy's good-natured, reliable presence so much so that when she took ill at the beauty parlor in the 1987, she had the salon owner call Daddy. It was Daddy, the son-in-law she had originally slapped with sharp-tongued comments, who cleaned her up after she vomited into the commode at the beauty shop. It was Daddy who drove her to the emergency room. And as she courted death, it was her once-spurned son-in-law who called her children to tell them she had been admitted to the hospital.

Throughout his lifetime, Daddy's good heart and congenial nature allowed him to coexist with all kinds of people, including Nanny. While he wasn't a vengeful man, it must have given him a little pleasure to know that Nanny had to eat her wicked words: "Well, now that you've got her, you can divorce her in a few months."

Mel and Molly Johnson were married for sixty-two years, six months, and four days—"'til Death did them part."

6

"LORDY! LORDY!"

"Go where your best prayers take you."
—Frederick Buechner

"Beyond the sunset, oh blissful morning...." Melody and words blended together as they danced out of the little house at the top of the hill. On any given day, you could hear the piano and Maw-Maw's enthusiastic, country-gospel rendition of some of her most beloved hymns.

"Beyond the sunset, oh blissful morning,
  When with our Savior, Heaven is begun,
  Earth's toiling ended. Oh, glory dawning!
  Beyond the sunset, when day is done!"

"Beyond the Sunset" may have been one of her favorites, but she knew many hymns. She would flip through her well-used songbook and accompany herself while she sang. Maw-Maw sang with zeal, her voice scooping and slurring notes with enthusiasm. Our high-school choir director, Mrs. Lewis, would have been appalled at my grandmother's utter disregard for hitting a note cleanly on the first attempt. Her rule was that you could *never* slide to find the note, and I often thought that if I had learned to sing by Maw-Maw's example, I would have received an F in chorus from our strict, but beloved choral teacher. Maw-Maw, however, was not directed by Lynn Lewis, but by an even higher power. She sang from the heart, not so much for the exact rendition of the notes, but for the offering up of faith to a God who loved the music of His child.

Maw-Maw, Marguerite Keach Johnson, played the piano the same way she sang—with more gusto than accuracy. Try it and you'll find out that simultaneously playing the piano and singing the lyrics takes considerable skill. She may have been far from concert-level, but she could sure pack a wallop, a talent to be admired. The songs she sang sunk into me like water into sand, so deep that the words and melodies flow without effort half a century later. "I come to the garden alone / While the dew is still on the roses / And the voice I hear /Falling on my ear /The Son of God discloses..../ And he walks with me, / and he talks with me / And he tells me I am his own, / And the joy we share as we tarry there / None other, can ever know."

Daddy couldn't play the piano by note like his mother could, but he did play "by ear," an ability that none of his three daughters possessed. Playing by ear is a magical, rare gift granted by God, and no two people play the same. Daddy had his own style, a lyrical smooth style, a la Perry Como or Frank Sinatra, but he claimed he could play a song only if he knew its lyrics. Some link in his brain connected the words of a song to finding the chords with his fingers. Once, at Daddy's sister's house, Aunt Evelyn played the piano for us, and I was amazed at the difference between the two siblings.

My aunt's "by-ear" style had a honky-tonk quality with a stronger rhythm and brighter touch than Daddy produced with his rambling fingers. I watched in awe as Aunt Evelyn's hands rose high above the keyboard after striking the keys, like she was a marionette with strings on her arms being lifted by a master puppeteer. (Which, in a sense, she was.) Whatever musical gene was passed from Maw-Maw, it flowed through the blood of her daughter and her son.

Maw-Maw's house was magical, all fun, freedom, and play. Standing in Maw-Maw's backyard and looking back to the right, there was a house where my favorite playmate lived. To this day I smile when I think of Scotty Spoonmore and his white-blond cocker spaniel named Goldie. Not having any brothers, Scotty was the first boy I ever hung around. Petting the ever-present, loyal Goldie, who never left Scotty's side, was my first experience with a dog. In those few early years, something more than a canine consciousness developed. Deep within my psyche the first tiny seed of gender awareness began to grow. Running around in my grandmother's yard with this neighborhood boy felt different than playing outside with my sisters.

One hot day in the summer of my sixth year, Scotty Spoonmore and I picked up hundreds of Rose-of-Sharon blossoms that had fallen along Maw-Maw's driveway where a long row of the bushes had dropped their spent blooms. Laying those damp, grayish-purple flower capsules end to end, Scotty bragged, "I'm making us a path to China."

"Really? You can go do that? Isn't that a *really* long way away? Like miles?" I asked as I continued to line up my dead flowers to finish the big loop that went down the driveway, outside the hedge at the front of the yard, and circled back into the side yard. "Can you really do that?"

Even as a child, I questioned the grandiose claims of the opposite sex. I didn't want to upset Scotty, but how could a boy in Indiana get us all the way to the other side of the globe? No matter how sure he acted, he couldn't really know the way to a foreign country, could he? Something wasn't right. But it was easier to make-believe he could lead us to China than to voice my doubts, so together, we laid routes in the grass made with wilted flowers. Together, we paved a passage to the other side of the world until my parents made me go home to reality.

Another evening, after a family dinner, Scotty Spoonmore and I were wandering the yard as the evening began to cool. Picnic tables had been set up in the backyard and all the adults were gathered around them, talking and enjoying the evening. Scotty and I wandered into the side yard, out of view of the picnickers. Bushes as big as trees, fat, tall, and green, lined the edge of Maw-Maw's yard where the garage cut into the sloping ground below. Wandering around those bushes, carefully walking on the ledge above the garage, we discovered a treasure. Those bushes had berries on them, all within easy reach—giant, juicy, and purple. As tempting as candy just waiting to be picked.

No talking was necessary. No giggling. No running. We were too busy picking and devouring, focused like bears on a honey stash.

After our foraging spree, Scotty and I ambled out of the berry bushes to where the grown-ups were sitting in the backyard. A gasp, then laughter, erupted from the group. Mother jumped up from her chair and marched towards us, gritting her teeth and growling low like a dog. "Missi-Ann!" (You always know you're in trouble when they use your middle name.) "What have you done, young lady?" she muttered sternly as she grabbed my hand and pulled me away from Scotty. Lucky for me there were other people around or Mother's disapproval would have been more obvious, probably involving several swats of her hand on my bare legs. I don't remember how Scotty looked, but purple stains mottled my pink-ruffled sundress, a crime against clothes and my mother. Magenta smears covered my face and blotches of berry mush smudged my legs and arms. Worse than that, I was absolutely covered with huge, red, angry welts from the mosquitoes that had fed on my juiced-up blood.

Too excited about the delicacy I was consuming, I hadn't noticed that hordes of insects were consuming me. Arms. Legs. Neck. Cheeks. Belly. I itched for days, miserable in the aftermath of my berry-binge and glad that Mother forgave me enough to dope me with Baby Aspirin and spray my entire body with Bactine.

Maw-Maw's house was on "Johnson Lane," named that because my Grandfather originally owned the land in that area, and because from the 1940's to the 1980's, at least one family of Johnson descendants lived on that section of ground. The white-clapboarded, square house that my grandmother lived in had been my grandparents' vision of down-sizing in the late 1940's. The structure featured a glassed-in porch.

One of the magical joys of Maw-Maw's house was the white wicker swing that hung at the end of that porch. When you opened the door to come in, that swing beckoned as surely as if it were talking. It lured me in with whispers: "Jump on. I'm waiting for you. We'll have fun." Temptation of unbounded bliss.

Maw-Maw was usually sitting on it, her wrinkled face bursting into a smile at the sight of one of her grandchildren come to visit. "Well, Missi-Dissi," she would croon, her playfulness with words a rhyming song that delighted my ears. She would clap her hands together in one extended grasp, a characteristic gesture that years after Daddy emulated in just the same way. Her eyes were always smiling from between the crow's feet wrinkles at the outside edge, and she was always saying things like "Isn't it a bea-u-ti-ous day?"

Swinging with Maw-Maw made me happy. Sometimes she would sing or we would make up little rhymes like "Missi-Ann, old tin can," or we would talk about all the things that grandmas and little girls talk about. Sometimes we would just swing in silence.

For the first five years of my life, my parents lived in a cracker-box white house at 155 Johnson Lane, just down the road from Maw-Maw. My sisters and I often walked up to visit with her. If she ever minded those random visits from grandchildren unannounced, she never let on. Maw-Maw was always happy to see us, inviting us to join her in whatever task she was working on at the moment.

One day I watched her mash berries through an aluminum, cone-shaped colander, a "sieve" she called it. As a kid, I had very little idea of what she was doing, especially since Mother didn't like to cook and nothing remotely like a "sieve" existed at our house. I stared at Maw-Maw's capable hands, awed by the dark purple mess that oozed through the holes of the sieve at her command. Another time, she sat me down next to her on the swing and said, "You're going to help me break beans." We sat on either side of a big metal bowl, snapping those crisp green pods as we gently swung on the front porch. Now, after seeing dozens just like that it in vintage markets, I know Maw-Maw's bean bowl was just an old aluminum container with nicks and dents and years of patina, but as a child, it was a shiny, silver, special vessel.

If Maw-Maw hadn't actually been in the middle of a chore when we showed up on her doorstep, she would bring out the Chinese Checkers, pulling the metal, star-painted board out from under her couch, and my sisters and I would squeal about which color to choose as our own. Hours would pass as we worked to get our marbles to the top of our star.

(All the Johnson girls have a competitive streak, and even a Chinese checker contest was worthy of fierce attention.)

The love of words and rhyme and the very music of speech was evident in Maw-Maw because she loved to learn and recite poems, "from memory." At a family reunion, Maw-Maw stood at the front of her living room, packed with various cousins and kin, and performed a recitation of a very long poem about "Jonah and the Whale." Her voice rose and fell. She fell silent with dramatic pauses. Her voice raced when Jonah was swallowed. Her tone trembled when Jonah deliberated and rose when he repented in the belly of the whale. Shouts rang through the living room when Jonah was spewed out in one mighty heave of the whale's stomach. More than a little afraid, my body would tremble. Poor, misbehaving Jonah was in the dark, smelly, belly of that whale only to be spit out as whale vomit.

Maw-Maw must have been a mighty orator because, let me tell you, I believed!

She often enacted recitations and programs like this at the fundamentalist, tiny Church of God she attended where everyone was addressed as "Brother" or "Sister." Card-playing was a sin, prayer meetings were constant, revivals were frequent, and talk of being saved was a daily occurrence.

Once in a while, Maw-Maw would say something about the "divan," and an absolute epiphany lit my brain upon realizing that the word "divan" was another word for "couch." Maw-Maw's couch was a taupe-velour type fabric with deep burgundy roses on it. I was fascinated not with the color or the print but with the trim that hung from the frame of the couch at the bottom all the way around. It was a taupe-gray, soft but heavy braid, each strand about four inches long. I remember sitting on the floor braiding it, playing with it, stroking it, awareness never dawning that my grandmother might not want her couch embellishments knotted up into strands.

One time, I was sick and staying with Maw-Maw until my parents could pick me up after they got off work. Maw-Maw had situated me on the "divan" with an "afghan." Being sick, I didn't feel like doing anything, so I counted the knot-holes in the pine paneling, which were supposed to be there, but which—even at a very young age—I found objectionable from a decorating standpoint. To this day, I am disgusted by any wood paneling that has knotholes in it.

Not only did Maw-Maw have a special swing, she had a "pass-through" window between the kitchen and the living room. That window-in-the-wall was the coolest thing ever. A huge, cushy chair sat right under the pass-through. Phone books and paper pads multiplied uncontrolled there around the heavy, black, circle-dial phone sitting on the left arm of the chair. Scrawled phone numbers cavorted in pen and pencil marks, flinging themselves willy-nilly, vertical, horizontal, and curved around the corners of scraps of paper. Dozens of notes, some with shorthand hieroglyphics that Maw-Maw learned from Business School in the 1920's, were stuffed inside the phone book. Bits of words like alphabet debris hovered above that chair where Maw-Maw used words instead of numbers at the beginning of a phone call. "Whitehall 5230. Hickory 8322," she'd mumble, her finger stuck in the dial like a pole in a hole. Some kind of secret code, I was sure, and I'd listen carefully as Maw-Maw chatted with her friend, Alma, while keeping her worn Bible under her left elbow the whole time.

Not a day went by when Maw-Maw wouldn't read her Bible, mouthing the words as she read. That precious book had a black cover, torn and crinkled, with the edges and hunks of the cover showing brown fabric underneath. Maw-Maw's Bible featured the words of Jesus emphasized in red ink, an important feature to my grandmother since she wanted to know exactly what Jesus had said and live her life accordingly. Every page in that Bible had pencil underlinings and notes in the margins. It was only fitting that above the pass-through over Maw-Maw's chair was a picture of Jesus praying. Wrapped in a tan tunic, hands folded in prayer, Jesus knelt in the middle of a dark path, an image that Maw-Maw understood and emulated.

Such faith. Such adherence to the Word. Her Bible was her guide, her comfort, her strength. After Maw-Maw died, Daddy gave her Bible to me. In addition to the frequent underlinings, the printed red text, and the notes in the margins that said things like, "Amen" "Hallelujah" and "Pray more," there is a note scrawled in Maw-Maw's handwriting inside the front cover: "I have a $20 bill inside my Sunday shoes." Did that mean she had emergency money? That she was reminding herself because she was forgetful? That it was an extra offering for church? That she knew God would protect it until she needed it? That handwritten note was evidence that Maw-Maw's faith was rooted in both the daily *and* the divine, and it makes her Bible that much more precious.

Treasures existed in Maw-Maw's kitchen, too, like the cookie jar made to look like a squirrel. His name was, according to Maw-Maw, "Earl." He was brown, had buck-teeth, and flaunted yellow painted trim on his apron. When Maw-Maw told me, "Help yourself to a cookie, Missi-Dissi," I'd lift off his head and reach inside his fat stomach. Earl-the-Squirrel's belly was always full of cookies that made my greedy fingers glad. Some had marshmallow innards covered with golden-colored icing. Or vanilla sandwich cookies filled with sweet white cream. Or pink and brown and orange sugar wafers that made my tongue tickle.

Maw-Maw was a good country cook in an era when

people didn't worry about how much bacon fat they consumed. Her fried chicken was mouth-watering, hot-dripping, crispy on the outside and steamy on the inside, good. It sounds cliched to say your grandmother's fried chicken is the best you've ever eaten, but it was. When I was seven, I asked Maw-Maw to write down her recipe for fried chicken so Mother could replicate it. There was nothing special about her recipe at all. No fancy ingredients or painstaking techniques. Instead, Maw-Maw's recipe mixed "a dollop" of flour, a "smidgeon" of paprika, a "sprinkling" of pepper, and a "smattering" of salt. She dipped each piece of chicken in egg, rolled it in the flour mixture, and then deep-fried it in a six-inch deep, heavy iron skillet filled to the brim with grease. My Mother, bless her heart, would never in her life use that much oil, nor would she create any food that wasn't overcooked to crispy, crunchy, or well-done, so asking for the recipe proved to be a wasted effort. (Mother always worried that if we didn't cook meat to smithereens, we might get "trichinosis.")

When Maw-Maw cooked supper for the family it was fried chicken with mashed potatoes, (real ones, peeled, boiled, and pulverized with a hand smasher—that funny gadget that looked like a curvy metal mountain road). Sliced tomatoes and peas had a place of honor on the table. "Set the table, Missi-Dissi," she would command, and I would carefully pick up her pretty Peach Depression glass dishes stacked on an open shelf. Her gray-Formica-topped table glowed pastel after I arranged the humble silverware and paper napkins around the sunset-shade-of-peach plates.

After dinner, Maw-Maw would treat us to her own special kind of dessert: fresh berries. We'd take spoonfuls of raspberries, blackberries, or strawberries, cover them with sugar, and drown them with milk. A certain joy existed in slurping syrupy, fuchsia-colored liquid from the bottom of a peach-colored bowl. No matter how old I am, berries and milk are a nostalgic treat that jolt me back to a childhood where a wrinkly, white-haired, smiling grandmother served me sweet things.

Before we opened our mouths to eat, we bowed our heads in prayer, Maw-Maw's faith so tangible we could feel it hovering in the air as she spoke. Her prayers were direct, first-hand conversations with a God she knew on a personal basis. Never prescribed, never pre-planned, they were instead a heartfelt talk to God about his presence in her daily life. She thanked him for the food before us. She asked blessings on those around her. She used people's first names and asked for healing or comfort or whatever that person needed. She prayed fervently for peace and often alluded to the fact that the end of the world was near. (As a child, I was both fascinated and frightened by Maw-Maw's talk to God, on one hand feeling God was right there with us, and on the other, fearing that I would be dying with the rest of the evil world that day.) Maw-Maw's prayers were long, a stark contrast to the prescribed daily blessing that we said at our house—"God is great. God is good, and so we thank him for our food." When Daddy prayed, he might add the phrase, "Lord, guide us and protect us," and would sometimes add a few direct requests for the special needs of friends or family. While Daddy's faith was sincere, he couldn't pray like my Maw-Maw. Few people could.

Father Pete, as Daddy's best friend, had known Maw-Maw for years. A priest who devoted his life to God, he had certainly heard thousands upon thousands of prayers. Every time he heard Maw-Maw pray, he would smile and humbly shake his head. "Mel, your Mother's prayers are the best I have ever witnessed. The most sincere, most potent prayers I've ever heard. The first time I heard her pray, it was traumatic for me. Nothing like the Hail Mary's and Rosaries that

I was used to. I have no doubt that she's actually having a conversation with God. She has a direct line in."

My child's adoration of Maw-Maw was just that: a child's love. While Daddy and Maw-Maw had a close bond, it was not a perfect relationship.

A couple of times a week on the way home from an errand, Daddy would drive the car to Johnson Lane and head to the house on the hill. One warm afternoon we arrived only to find the house empty. Daddy started running when smoke appeared from the back yard. He skidded to a halt when he saw a wiry, old, wrinkle-faced woman standing next to a black kettle swinging from a tripod. Underneath it, a raging fire crackled. Orange flames licked the sides of the cauldron, glowing red with gray embers bursting upward like fireworks. If I hadn't known any better, I would wonder if Maw-Maw was a witch, reminiscent of crazy Aunt Jean who kept dead cats as familiars.

Daddy's face was red as he ran toward her. "Mother! What are you doing? You're going to catch your yard on fire!"

Even through the smoke, I could see Maw-Maw scowl. "Now, Melly!" she barked. "I know what I'm doing. I've been making lye soap since before you were born!"

It was the only time I ever heard Maw-Maw speak sharply.

Daddy mumbled, once again a boy rebuked by his mother. "Well, I could have at least helped you haul the pot out of the barn."

In 1966, Maw-Maw had cataract surgery to remove the clouds from her eyes. Frightened by the large eye patch she wore when she came home, I hovered behind my parents as they checked on her each day after surgery. A few days post-op we were in her living room when Maw-Maw startled me by exclaiming, "Well, praise be, Missi! Your shirt has blue and

BRIGHT green!" She smiled broadly and clapped her hands so they grasped each other. That was when I realized Maw-Maw hadn't even been able to see me for a long time. Until I outgrew it, that cobalt-blue skirt and sweater outfit with two stripes of apple-green running down each side became my favorite thing to wear. It had, in my mind, brought me back to her.

On July 20th, 1969, our family gathered in the cramped den, Daddy and Maw-Maw on one couch, Mother on the other, and the three girls scattered around the room. From my perch on the edge of the brick hearth, I watched Maw-Maw's face as Neil Armstrong's foot dropped from the Apollo ladder and onto the dust of the moon. Wonder shone from each wrinkle and pore. Her eyes sparkled. She clasped her callused hands together in a gesture of pure delight before crowing, "Lordy, Lordy! A man on the moon! Whoever would have thunk it?"

For someone born in a previous century, witnessing a man stepping on the face of the moon was a miracle. To commemorate the occasion, Daddy served us homemade ice cream filled with chocolate shavings, then-and-there dubbed "Apollo" ice cream. We ate big bowls of the delicacy as we witnessed history and praised modern moon exploration.

After Maw-Maw's eyesight began to irreversibly fail, she had a car accident. She didn't tell us. Turns out, Maw-Maw thought she could hide the damage. A "can-do" kind of gal, she took a not-exactly-matching can of spray paint and buzzed it over the side of the car. Daddy quickly deduced what had happened. It wasn't hard. Parked under the carport, her turquoise car flaunted a massive, darker smear of blue paint along the side. At that point my parents began to worry that Maw-Maw might not need to be driving. Shortly after the "I'll-paint-the-car-blue" episode, during a family gathering in Maw-Maw's basement, she poured a family member a drink of anti-freeze, believing it was Kool-Aid. From that point on, Daddy was *certain* that she shouldn't drive. She needed supervision and help at home.

One of my first and most painful lessons about life failing was seeing Maw-Maw come out of the bathroom, a slimy turd attached to the heel of her shoe. Totally unaware of her predicament, she asked, "Now, whose house is this?" in the home my parents had lived in for more than twenty years. Daddy and his siblings agonized about finding Maw-Maw a place to live. Before long, she moved into a room at Providence Nursing Home in New Albany. The old house on Johnson Lane, swing and pass-through included, was sold to strangers, and for the first time in decades, not one Johnson family descendant lived on that portion of ground.

Maw-Maw had always said she was ready to see the good Lord. Anyone who had ever heard her pray knew that she was looking forward to the reunion with her "mighty, all-powerful God," words she used often in her prayers. When she fell at the nursing home at the age of ninety and broke her hip, she gave up, died peacefully, and was warmly welcomed to that glowing, peaceful place "Beyond the Sunset" she had so often sung about.

PRECIPITOUS BIRTH

"Dad and I went back to our house and cut the grass, mowed the high weeds, and cleaned out the fence row. It's beginning to look real neat. Honey, I'll be so glad when we get settled in that little white house. How could anyone help but be happy?"
—Letter to Molly, June 4, 1952

"Mel, Mel, help me!" Mother screamed from the bathroom. "Somewhere between the fantasy of a dream and a reality," Daddy would pen years afterward, "I heard Molly's urgent cry. Still in the distant fog, the cry again, and then reality struck home, and with a bolt-like action, I sprang out of bed." (His re-telling makes himself sound a little like a superhero bounding up and ready for anything.)

It was September 5th, 1960, Melanie's seventh birthday, a day that lives in infamy in the Johnson Family Chronicles.

The night before, as Mother leaned over to kiss her good-night, Melanie whined, "Mother, I want the new baby to be born on my birthday. Can you, please?"

"Oh, it doesn't look like you're going to get your wish, Melanie," Mother said, her gentle voice reassuring despite delivering bad news.

Since she was two weeks overdue, she should have known not to make promises.

Daddy often recounted the events to us, polishing the story to a diamond in the Johnson-tale-trove.

"That night I heard your Mother yelling. I stumbled into the bathroom, and there she sat, perched on the toilet, groaning."

"'Aaagghhh. Ugggh. Mel! Meeeeellllllll!'" Daddy made his voice deep and throaty, groaning out the words himself to show us how Mother sounded.

"What in the world was I supposed to do?" he asked. "After all, I was just a guy. I wasn't having the baby. I was only a bystander when it came to the arrival of a new baby."

"So I told myself just as soon as this pain subsides, we'll rush to the hospital. We've been through this twice before. No use to get panicky."

"Well, let me tell you, girls. Not panicking was easier said than done, no matter what I planned!" Daddy chopped the air with his hands.

"Before I could do anything, Mother shrieked out a ferocious plea. '"Oh, God! Help me!'" she yelled, "followed by a loud thud."

Daddy paused dramatically as he waited for the impact of his words to sink in.

We all knew that only extreme terror or unfathomable pain would cause my reserved, prim Mother to scream out the Lord's name. The ominous "thud" resounded through our minds.

"Your Mother was wailing, 'The baby's here! The baby's

here!' and I was sure that from the terrible sound of the thud, our baby was dead." Daddy's tone was somber now.

"But, you know, girls. You do what you have to do. So with one hand, I lifted Mother up off the commode. She kinda stood there on wobbly legs..." Here, Daddy shifted his body from one side to the other to demonstrate Mother's shaky stance. "Then, with the other hand, I fished the baby out of the toilet. I couldn't believe it. That baby was alive and looked totally fine. Her fall from the womb was cushioned by the water of the toilet bowl."

While Daddy was always careful not to get too gory and give too many graphic details, we were all aware that this was a night that could traumatize and scar someone forever. This fact, however, never stopped Melanie and I from laughing about the story of Michele's birth. Daddy, too, was relatively unscathed by the traumatic event and loved to tell the story. Mother never said anything, and just kept her mouth in a straight line. *She* was traumatized.

"I was just getting ready to administer a whack across the rump like I had seen the doctor do in movies when the baby took several gasps and let forth with the most wonderful sound I'll ever hear—a lusty cry of life. But then I've got this baby, and there's blood and a cord, and..." Daddy's voice tapered off before resuming animatedly.

"I yelled to Melanie, who was just turning seven. 'Call Maw-Maw! Hurry!'"

Melanie was used to dialing her grandmother's phone number, but that night, hovering on the edge of crisis and scared by the intensity of Daddy's voice and the sounds and smells coming from the bathroom, her shaking fingers couldn't get the heavy dial to push all the way up to the stop. She tried several times, but she just couldn't get the call to go through.

"Daddy! I can't do it! It won't work!" Melanie was crying. Terrified.

"That's when I handed Mother the slippery, squealing baby, and dialed 0," Daddy recounts. "As soon as the operator came on, I sputtered, 'The baby's here! The baby's here! What do I do? What do I do? Get me the doctor!'"

"Lucky for me, the woman on the phone knew what she was doing," Daddy explained. "Soon a drowsy male voice cut through my mounting panic. 'Tie the cord in two places and cut in the middle,' the doctor barked out. Then I heard him ordering the operator to dispatch the sheriff to 155 Johnson Lane. IMMEDIATELY! Then he told me he'd see me at the hospital."

Daddy's next move was to slam the phone into the receiver and rush to the kitchen to look for scissors.

"Good luck with that," I chuckled under my breath as I listened. Mother *always* hid the scissors. She'd owned the same pair since she went to nursing school in 1949 and believed them to be the best scissors ever made, a pair so spectacular they couldn't possibly be placed in the hands of non-medical personnel or, heaven forbid, be used for dirty, unhallowed pursuits. Mother was afraid her children would cut paper with her holy scissors, or worse yet, take them outside and lose them. For most of our young lives, it was impossible to find anything other than a dull paring knife in my mother's kitchen.

Imagine. A newborn baby has just landed headfirst in your toilet, your wife is in distress, and you are frantically searching for a pair of scissors. Daddy describes tossing everything from the kitchen cabinet drawers onto the floor, throwing willy-nilly paper clips, coupons, dishrags, serving spoons, and pencils. Finally, his bloody hands landed on his familiar garden shears and a loose piece of wrapping cord.

"I rushed back to the bathroom," Daddy continued. "Your

Mother was in a semi-state of shock, still holding the baby. My hands were quivering so bad I wasn't sure I could cut the cord, but I did. I snipped it in half with my oversized, outdoor garden clippers, gasping, 'Look, Molly. We have a little boy!'"

"'Mother shook her head. 'You'd better look again, Mel. We have another girl.'"

"And yes, Michele, you were *a girl!*" Daddy beamed at his youngest daughter. He must have wondered how he could have made such an obvious mistake. No doubt the mess and the mayhem had clouded his brain.

"By this time, I had the presence of mind to call my parents," Daddy remembered. "'Come quick! I need help!'"

Since they lived just up the road, Maw-Maw and Paw-Paw appeared within minutes.

"'Mother!' I shouted when I ran into the living room, baby in my arms. 'Do you know anything about delivering a baby?'"

Horrified, he watched as Maw-Maw threw up her hands and wailed, "Melford, I don't know a thing about delivering babies!" just like the howling Prissy in *Gone with the Wind*.

"When the Sheriff arrived, he was grateful the baby had already been born because he'd been afraid that he was going to have to deliver the baby. Instead, all he had to do was whisk us off to the hospital. Later, the doctor found me in the waiting room and congratulated me on perfecting a tightly-tied cord. I guess my knot-tying as an Eagle Scout and Navy training really have kicked in!" Daddy laughed.

The doctor shook Daddy's hand. "Your baby weighs seven pounds, two ounces. Everything is fine with your wife and your daughter, but they will be in isolation during their stay because of the 'contaminated' delivery of the precipitous birth."

Michele Lauren Johnson was born that eventful day, on

Melanie Beth Johnson's seventh birthday, and the rest, as they say, is history.

The event that night was a "precipitous birth," as Daddy recorded in his typewritten story, titled "Baby in a Hurry." Precipitous means "rash, hasty, or to throw headlong..." My younger sister arrived so quickly, without providing Mother any labor pains, (no wonder Mother liked her best!) that Mother sat on the toilet and Michele plopped out. You can imagine, can't you, the cruel yet witty jokes my sister has borne all her life because of the unusual circumstances of her birth? "Swam like a fish from the day she was born" and "Rushing head first into things" were a few of the kindest Melanie and I would taunt. "Toilet Baby" was one of the least.

"What a sight to behold!" Daddy would quip as he finished the story. "I looked at myself in the waiting room mirror. Old pair of faded Bermuda shorts, an old sports shirt, and no shoes. I was splattered from head to foot." (Those who love him just grin because with the exception of the blood smatters, most of his later wardrobe consisted of exactly that: old faded Bermuda shorts, an old sports shirt, and no shoes.)

"I celebrated the delivery of our third daughter by totally breaking down and having a good cry by myself, seen only by my own disheveled reflection in the waiting room mirror."

Billions of men have been fathers over time. Millions of men have been loving role models through the centuries. Hundreds of thousands of men have been present at the birth of their child. But precious few men have delivered their own baby. On that particular night, only a man named Melford was there to help a woman named Molly give birth in the bathroom of a tiny house at the end of Johnson Lane. Only one special Daddy brought my sister, Michele, the third and final Johnson girl, into the world.

8

THUMBELINA, DANCE!

"Nothing that grieves us can be called little: by the eternal laws of proportion
a child's loss of a doll and a king's loss of a crown
are events of the same size."
—Mark Twain

Daddy killed Thumbelina.

"Oh, Missi, I'm so sorry! I'll take her to the doctor and get her fixed. I promise. Right away. She'll be back and good as new in no time!" Daddy was doing everything he could to placate me.

"But Daddy! I didn't even get to play with her," I moaned, chin quivering.

The little white plastic cradle wasn't rocking and wasn't filled with my baby.

Daddy's earnest apology and chagrined face didn't do a lot to ease my sorrow. I had barely gotten her unwrapped and had just started to hold and rock her that Christmas morning before Daddy excitedly said, "Miss, let me show you how she works. She moves her head and arms just like a real baby."

Reluctantly, I handed over my own personal bundle of joy, never suspecting the tragic outcome.

Daddy turned her over and put his big hand over the round knob on her back while he talked. "It's really neat," he said giving her knob a full rotation.

"What toys can do nowadays!" He grinned at me and turned the dial again.

"She nods her head and moves her arms." Daddy held her up in front of me and then he cranked that knob two more rotations for good measure.

"Missi, Thumbelina feels like a real baby!" Daddy beamed as he wound that wheel yet another couple of turns.

"Daddy! Let me do it!" I was nearly bursting with excitement over my new baby doll.

Daddy, however, just couldn't let go.

Winding the knob on Thumbelina's back one more time to ensure she'd be gyrating enough when I got to hold her, he held her out to me.

My waiting arms were reaching desperately for my new baby, ready to welcome her into my life when a noise shrieked out of her. A terrible, strangling, popping moan hung in the cinnamon-scented air of Christmas morning.

Thumbelina would not move again that day...or for several months after.

Daddy had singlehandedly popped the plaything I wanted most, literally robbing the cradle. He felt horrible. I was sad, mad, and disappointed, a five-year-old whose wounded soul became Daddy's first priority that Christmas morning. Taking care of Thumbelina became his second.

The day after Christmas, Daddy chauffeured Thumbelina all the way across Louisville to a toy store a long way from home. He laughed when the manager admitted to him, "Yep. there are probably a hundred Thumbelinas in need of a doll doctor today. However, sir," the manager quipped, "most of the patients at our toy hospital were wound up too tight by excited little girls, not by their excited fathers."

A couple of months later, Thumbelina finally returned home, and I was glad to see her. Sort of. After the crisis of that Christmas morning, I was a little afraid of her. Even with her new, working knob and her pretty eyes, she reminded me that she could explode from the inside-out at any moment. I worried that I would kill my own baby in some kind of psychotic winding spree.

Thumbelina never again held the same charm for me that she had in that first instant I saw her on Christmas morning, right after she was unwrapped and placed in my arms, sweet and unmutilated. I wanted her the most right before Daddy got hold of her.

I only wished I could have loved her as much as he had.

9

THE THANKSGIVING WITCH

"If a cat spoke, it would say things like, 'Hey, I don't see the problem here."
—Roy Blount, Jr.

Daddy pounded on the peeling wooden door for at least two minutes calling, "Aunt Jean! Aunt Jean! It's Mel. I've brought you some Thanksgiving dinner."

I was terrified. I just knew that the house would fall down around us if Daddy knocked any harder. The little house drooped in the center, like it had given up all hope. Peeling paint. Boarded windows. Everything was gray. This was like nothing I'd ever seen before and had only heard of in ghost stories.

The door cracked open, revealing just a slice of skin with part of an eye at the top.

Deep rumbles of scratchy noise. "Melford, is that you?"

I shrank back as the door swung open, exposing an ugly, old woman. Her crackly, low voice scared me almost as much as her appearance. Gray, frizzy hair grew straight out of her wrinkly head, as if she were some strange wizened porcupine. She was so skinny I was afraid her brittle body would crack into pieces, just like the sugar bowl I had once dropped on the kitchen floor. I pictured this woman lying in shards on the decaying wooden porch.

My eyes blurred with tears of terror when she began to shuffle toward us.

Huddled behind Daddy, my hands tightened on the package I was carrying. Not that cellophane-wrapped Styrofoam would provide any protection, but it was something to grip in the midst of my panic.

Daddy's gentle, "Come on, Miss," forced me to follow behind him, dragging my feet every step of the way as Aunt Jean led us into her front room.

Three steps in and my hand involuntarily smacked my nose. A horrible, nasty, stingy smell floated around the room. My eyes watered and my throat tightened. I wanted to cough and wave my hands around, but I was holding that darn package. Why wasn't Daddy flinching and running? Why had we come here to this awful place? My brain screamed, "I don't care if she is related to us. She's a witch!"

In the deteriorating family homestead of this distant aunt, out in a country field in the middle of nowhere, all the rooms had been closed off and moved into one. Aunt Jean's front room was her only room. Old furniture cluttered each inch of wall space. Trash covered every surface. Piles of old, yellow newspapers occupied all available floor space. Brown paper grocery bags were stuffed with garbage and crammed into the room. We couldn't even walk in more than a few steps. Not that I wanted to.

Everywhere were piles of junk and bags of trash. But that wasn't the only horror. Lurking behind those sacks, everywhere I looked, was a skinny, motley cat. Pairs of green and gold eyes blinked erratically in the gloom. Striped. Calico. Tabby. White. Orange. Brown. And of course, solid black. What witch wouldn't have a black cat?

Even more overwhelming than the filth of that room was the not-so-subtle scent. Forget Denmark. Something was definitely rotten in the hills of Southern Indiana.

My gaze raced around the room in both panic and fascination. Could this be real?

There, stretched out like a concrete statue on the greasy vinyl of an old dinette chair was a gray-striped cat in obvious rigor mortis.

"But Aunt Jean," Daddy coughed. "This cat is *dead!*"

"Melford!" Aunt Jean barked as she pointed a gnarly finger right at Daddy's chest in reprimand. "The cat says NO! It is NOT dead. It's only sleeping."

I must have been in shock. One dead cat had no more impact on me than the dozens of live cats skulking through the detritus of Aunt Jean's one-room abode. No memory exists for what Daddy said to Aunt Jean or how Daddy handled the cat corpse crisis, but I do recall wondering how fast we could give Aunt Jean our Thanksgiving offering and leave. The whole time I stood behind Daddy in that room, I devised escape routes and planned what I would do if Aunt Jean suddenly commanded me to come closer with a crook of her clawed finger.

Relief coursed through my veins when I could finally give up my box of wrapped food and have my hands free for protection. As I fled through the creaky wooden door, the maniacal whispering of Aunt Jean blended in with the howling of the cats around her ankles.

Daddy's departing words seemed unbelievable: "Take care of yourself, Aunt Jean. Have a good Thanksgiving."

On the way back home, fat tears coursed down my cheeks. I cried with relief, from the release of adrenalin, and because I had gotten my first taste of realism. Not everyone lived the nice life I did. I cried because I was mad. The old witch hadn't even said "Thank You."

Poor, crazy Aunt Jean floats like a Halloween ghoul through my memory every Thanksgiving. As a child, I could only be thankful to flee her stinky house and escape the harsh, unpleasant realities of life, so removed from my own loving, warm, odor-free, home. As an adult, I know about hoarding, aging, and mental illness. My fear of these very things causes me to avoid the kind of charity that Daddy so freely gave. His explanation of our visit to Aunt Jean echoes back. "Daddy, why did we even go there?" I sniffed.

"Because, Miss. There but for the grace of God, go I."

At the time it didn't make much sense. It wasn't like Daddy to say that he was glad she was like that instead of him, but later I began to understand what Daddy meant: We need to be concerned for others because we, too, may need compassion someday. Years from now, I may be just like Aunt Jean. Hopefully, my eccentricities and dementia won't keep a person from performing an act of kindness.

Daddy may have continued to visit Aunt Jean, but I never saw her again. She died not long after this incident, some other relative finding her stiff and cold, covered with cats.

To this day, I am grateful that everywhere in the world, no matter how bad things seem, people like Daddy teach the art of compassion by personal example. He demonstrated that acts of kindness don't have to be recognized by the recipient. True Thanksgiving, the instigator of good deeds, is felt in the heart of the giver.

10

GOING ON A BEAR HUNT

"I knew it would happen one of these days, still it took me by surprise. Congratulations, old boy!

Of course, I am expecting an invitation to the wedding. I won't be able to come but send me one anyway. I always wanted to be at your wedding. I wanted to see your face on that day of days, and to see the bride coming down the aisle, to hear you both say, "I do."
And I always dreamed of visiting with you, of talking, and laughing, and singing with you, (maybe getting a little mad at you now and then), of picnics and outings together. Such occasions are going to be rather rare I'm afraid, but I'll always be expecting a hearty welcome on Johnson Lane. (I wouldn't be surprised if the Johnson family started a little city up there.)

I knew that you would find the girl *one of these days. I was just wondering when it would be.*

You always wanted to go to Brazil, but I think you are in for a more thrilling adventure now—of loving, rearing a family,

working, planning, hoping, suffering. But I think you are well-prepared to accept the responsibilities."
—Letter from Paul Peterson to Mel, June 1, 1952

"**G**irls, I want you to get cleaned up and help your mother set the table because Father Pete is going to be here for dinner." We cheered and clapped our hands in delight. Michele bounced up and down in her seat. All three of us, Melanie, Melissa, and Michele, scampered to follow Daddy's orders.

"Oh, yea! Father Pete!"

"I *love* it when he comes!"

"Wonder what game we'll play this time?"

"When will he get here?"

My sisters and I rattled off our comments simultaneously, high-pitched, girly voices bouncing off the walls. Excitement burbled out of us and spilled into the kitchen as we gathered up the lunch dishes.

Melanie moaned slightly. "Do we have to make our rooms 'company clean'?" This was Mother's phrase for a drastic cleaning and immaculate presentation of our rooms—as if they would not only be visited by, but also inspected by guests. Father Pete was special, but even he didn't motivate us to "company-clean" our rooms.

"Will he play with us again?" Michele asked.

Daddy grinned. "Yes, I'm sure he will."

"Can we tell him about Moses?" I asked. Moses was the new addition to the family. Our first, ever pet. He was a big, blue-gray cat with kind olive eyes, and I loved him.

"Well, Miss. I'm pretty sure Father Pete already knows about Moses," Daddy said, making a theology joke way above my age level. "But you can show him our cat."

I was positive that Father Pete would love Moses like nobody else could. No one, absolutely no one, was like Father Pete.

He always reminded me of the kid on the cover of *MAD* magazine, for no other reason than because Father Pete had big ears and a big smile. He was not a redhead, did not have freckles, and did not have big teeth, so there really wasn't much of a resemblance, but it's hard to account for the ideas that bloom in a kid's mind.

To me, "Father Pete," was simply Daddy's best friend—a smiling, soft-spoken man who was a part of every holiday he could manage and a frequent presence in our family. Other than the black shirt with stiff white-collar band he wore, he seemed just like Daddy, smiling, laughing, and taking part in whatever ceremony, game, or event we were involved in. From the time I was a little girl, I was drawn to him, intrigued by him. We went to Centenary Methodist Church every week of my life, following my parents in their quiet, Protestant faith. We didn't understand Catholicism, so when Daddy talked about "Pete," it was only about his boyhood buddy, not a priest.

We didn't even know that calling him "Father Pete" seemed irreverent to others.

When I was six or seven, we attended some kind of Catholic service. Daddy's good friend, Bill Jamison, and his family were there, too, along with Father Pete. People all around me were making comments about "Father Paul" and "Father Peterson."

What two men were they talking about? I was totally confused.

Then, a brilliant, blinding, epiphany struck me, just like in cartoons when lightning strikes above someone's head. The people chatting around me, using a lot of "Father" names, weren't talking about two men, but one. "Father Pete has aliases!" I thought with surprise. "And we don't even call him those names." The Johnson girls were the only people in the world who would ever address this revered priest so flippantly as "Father Pete," a term coined by Daddy, combining Paul Peterson's boyhood nickname of "Pete" with the priestly term "Father."

From the minute Father Pete walked in the door of Driftwood Drive, we talked to him. (God gave him big ears, after all, so he could be a great listener.) Father Pete always asked questions, and he asked them as if your answers really mattered. They were probing questions, directly related to your life, no matter your age. "Melissa, tell me about what you're reading." "Tell, me, Melanie, about the music you're working on." "Michele, tell me about your plans for the summer." He was skillful at asking questions that couldn't be answered with "yes" or "no" because he was genuinely interested in you.

The after-dinner activities when Father Pete came to visit always included some kind of family fun. That particular evening, Father Pete took us on a "trip."

"Tonight, we're going on a bear hunt," Father Pete said, his eyes sparkling.

He gathered us in a circle. Our fannies filled every seat on the hearth and the two couches crammed into the tiny den. Even Mother and Daddy hurried to settle in. Who, after all, didn't want to go on a safari with Father Pete?

"We're going on a bear hunt... X marks the spot." Father Pete began to intone in a rhythmic cadence.

"We're going on a bear hunt, X marks the spot. Now clap your hands against your thighs as we walk so we know how far we're walking."

The entire Johnson clan slapped their hands against their legs, right, left, right, left, right, left, walking right along with Father Pete.

"Now we're going through some really tall grass," he explained. "I want you to rub your hands together real fast so it sounds like the rustle of grass."

Obediently, we all rubbed our hands together. Sure enough, it did sound like a herd of people going through the grass.

Father Pete talked quietly, looking around the circle and establishing eye contact with each and every person. "Now remember, we've got to get that bear so you're going to have to pick up the pace."

The rhythm of his hands speeded up. The even cadence became a fast stampede of hand slaps as we followed along.

"Oops. Stop! Look over there. There's water!" Father Pete pointed a long finger to the corner of the den.

"Now we've got to cross that big river so you're going to have to swim." Here, he crossed his arms in front of him, right arm, left arm, a dry freestyle that we could visualize. Soon we had all stopped the "running" of our hands on our legs and were instead swimming across the family room.

Father Pete's voice rose in fear. "Oh, no! On the other side of the river, there's mud. Deep, oily, thick mud! You've got to pick up your feet really high so you can move." Father Pete's feet stomped loudly and slowly. The army of Johnsons followed him, our footsteps making the figurines on the bookcases rattle.

"Wait. Look!" Father Pete stopped the heavy stomping. We all followed him, some of us stopping with knee still raised.

"What's there? I think it's a cave." Hand over his eyebrows like a lookout on a ship, Father Pete pointed toward the hidden hole somewhere far away through the kitchen door.

"We can't go over it. We can't go under it. We've got to go through it. But we *don't* want to scare the bats. You'll have to tiptoe." Suddenly, the twelve stomping feet in the room were all prancing tiptoes. Only the tips of our fingers tapped a light rhythm on our legs.

"AARRRRRAAAGHHHHH!" Father Pete growled. Fiercely.

We stop moving, a communal gasp of surprise.

Suddenly, he's screeching in panic. "OOOOH! There's a bear in the cave! Turn around! Go back! Go back!"

Father Pete's abrupt change in voice startled us. He had gone from whispering and "tiptoeing" to growling to screeching. We were squealing too, burbling with noises of shock, delight, and fear, following our fearless leader. Daddy was playing along with Father Pete, not wanting to be outdone, and every once in a while Mother would mutter a phrase like, "I'm just too slow!" "Wait a minute," or "Oh, for goodness' sakes!"

"Turn around! Go back. We've got to go back the way we came!" Father Pete directed us.

"Tiptoe through the cave!" he whispered urgently. The din in our den eased into the relative quiet of pattering fingers and tiptoeing feet.

Father Pete commanded, "Now, stomp through the mud!" Twelve feet pounded in various rhythms, trying to escape the gooey mud on the banks. Clomp. Clomp. Clomp.

"Swim through the river!" Father Pete shouted, and we obeyed. It's a wonder we didn't blind each other, sitting so close together, all those elbows flying as we swam imaginary, Olympic-paced laps across the deep river.

Faster and faster went Father Pete, repeating (forgive the "re-Pete" pun) all the gestures of our Bear Hunt, in reverse order. Our hands slapped our legs like footsteps. Our eyes watched every move he made. Our bodies mimicked what he did. Grunts and shouts and giggles reverberated through the house as we returned from our adventure, laughing, out-of-breath, and red-thighed.

On other visits, Father Pete would bring word games. He may have been the Johnson's original wiseman bearing a gift of the "Himindinger" game that we loved. Everyone got a sheet of paper and drew six columns on it. The group agreed on two things: categories to go in each column across the top, and then one six-letter word to go along the side, broken down into its individual letters. The object of the game was to fill every box with a legitimate answer. If your category across the top was "color," and you had the letter "f" from the word "friend" on the side, you'd have to come up with "fuchsia" in that box to get a point. (No wonder I grew up loving words. The more I knew, the better the chances of winning!)

Father Pete also played a game called "The Slaves of Old are Playing Koshengala," or at least that's what it sounded like to me. In that game, everyone sat on the floor and passed pop bottles around to the beat of the song that Father Pete sang. Part of the game was knowing when to reverse the movement and start clunking bottles around in the opposite direction. I have absolutely no recollection of the rules. Just the fun.

It was always fun when Father Pete came to our house. We were always sorry to see him leave, and we always looked forward to his next visit.

The memorable "Bear-Hunt" evening had been no exception. When Father Pete said his good-byes, he shook Daddy's hand and clapped a hand on his shoulder. He took Mother's hand in between his two, long slender hands and said, "Now, Molly. Try to keep Mel out of trouble. And take care of yourself, dear." Then he squatted down in the circle of girls and one cat that had gathered round him. "Girls, on my next visit, I want to hear all about what you've been up to. Okay? Keep up the good work. Be good for your parents, and thanks for playing the game with me. I really enjoyed that."

Grinning at us, Father Pete stood up, pausing just long enough to stroke Moses' big gray head. Even the cat smiled.

11

OF GOATS AND MEN

"My father didn't tell me how to live. He lived and let me watch him do it."
—Clarence Budington Kelland

"Molly, remember those shorts you tried to make for me? That were put together backward? I couldn't even get my leg into them because the seam pointed forward." Daddy threw up his hands in mock distress. Mother lowered her head, grimaced, and said, "I'm just not coordinated enough for sewing. All I ever remember was Mother telling me to rip it out, over and over again."

"Oh, Molly! It isn't that hard." Daddy laughed, shaking his head. While he wasn't cruel, he also had no qualms about teasing other people and Mother was a prime candidate because she so freely admitted that she couldn't do anything that took creativity.

Mother's lack of sewing ability was most obvious in the fall when Halloween rolled around. She didn't have the skills to make costumes, was too busy working, and was too conservative to want to dress us up as something wild. She ignored the upcoming holiday, fending off our costume requests with an evasive, "We'll see." While she loved clothes and was a champion shopper, to think of putting together an outlandish get-up was as far out of her comfort zone as becoming a professional basketball player. The mere idea of having to craft a cape or make a mask sent Mother into a tight-mouthed expression with an exasperated, "Oh, for goodness' sake!" Consequently, it was always Daddy who came up with the Halloween costumes. He did it with the same zeal as Maw-Maw singing at the piano.

You wouldn't think I'd be grateful for being made into a goat, but my first memory of Daddy making me a costume was just that. Daddy whispered to me, "I have something special to make this work," before he took to crafting a skinny shoe box into the shape of a head with a long snout. Using a compass and a pencil, he drew big curls on another sheet of cardboard. I watched in amazement as that heavy brown material became very believable horns when Daddy cut and stapled them onto the box. Alas, that shoe-box-snout-face was too narrow even for my kindergarten-sized head, and the staples that held the horns nearly lacerated my ears. So Daddy bent the box outward and glued globs of cotton balls inside where my ears were situated so that wearing the head wouldn't hurt. Whipping a can of white spray-paint off the old workbench in the basement, Daddy worked with a flourish, using his special magic to transform me into a baby satyr complete with goat ears and horns.

"Here's where the secret ingredient comes in," he mumbled to me as he pulled something out of a round, metal tin on his bench. In his palm were two huge, glass eyes of deep gold, complete with vertically shaped black pupils.

"Now, Miss, those are really good eyes. I got them special

from a man, and I've had them a long time." To this day, I don't know what he meant by that. Now I wish I would have asked Daddy about those crazy goat-peepers. Where in the world did he get them? What kind of man did he get them from? A taxidermist? A veterinarian? A lunatic optician? Truth be told, I was more than a little afraid of those luminous orbs and didn't want to look that Billy-goat in the eye. Cloaked in a white bath towel pinned at the neck, I bravely pulled on the head without confronting those eyes and went off to the kindergarten Halloween parade, where, at the age of five, I pranced around with pride, happy to be a goat.

In 1964, I was six years old and excited about the big Halloween gathering in the parking lot of McClures Drugstore, on the main drag of Clarksville. Daddy must have seen the poster advertising the event and thought it would be fun for us because he declared we were going. I knew about Michele's costume and was a little jealous when she got to be something cool and I was going to be something gross. That year, Daddy transformed me into an ugly old man. A man's red plaid flannel shirt covered my tiny body, making me look like a ninety-year-old shrunken man. Where Daddy got that mask that he handed me, I'll never know, but the plastic face was long and haggard, tinged with gray in the cheekbones and creased with wrinkles on the forehead.

Just by luck, the nose that projected from the mask lay on my lips, so whenever I moved my mouth, the nose lifted and snarled making the old man's face look animated. I couldn't see a thing unless I moved my head a certain way, and then I could only see with one eye through a tiny pinprick of a hole. At least fifty people that day pulled or poked the nose of that mask trying to see how it was wired. Whenever I sensed someone was near, I gyrated my mouth like a gymnast doing flips at the Olympics to make that mask dance.

Hundreds of kids were lined up in a long row in the

massive parking lot. Judges dressed in suits were walking up and down in front of each row, evaluating for prizes like, "Most Original," "Scariest," "Prettiest," "Ugliest." I was too young to know if they had age divisions and have no clue as to the exact categories. All I know is that of out of that legion of kids, I won the prize for the ugliest costume on the lot that day. My award? A brilliant, shiny, silver Kennedy half-dollar. I was rich! And I was glad the hot, sticky, suffocating underside of that mask hadn't made me quit trying to impress people.

Unfortunately, the prize money had a sad ending, but that's another story.

That same year, Daddy made Michele into an inanimate object. Taking his magic can of white spray-paint, he coated a big box after cutting a large hole in the top of it. A plastic tablecloth with a hole cut in exactly the same spot as the box, was glued to the top. He attached brightly-colored plastic plates and silverware to the top of the box on either side, like place-settings at a dinner party. Taking an orange plastic jack-o-lantern head, Daddy poked out the eyes and carved off the bottom and glued it over the hole in the box, creating a centerpiece. "Now, how's that for thinking outside the box? Of course, I couldn't table that idea," he punned. Even though I'd gained my costume glory winning the "ugly" award and in being the only goat Daddy ever made, I still felt pangs of jealousy when Michele got to be a table and won her own award for being the "most original."

When everybody else was being a princess, a hippie, a pirate, or a gypsy, the young Johnson girls were appearing as unique, hand-crafted curiosities. How many kids had fathers who were fun and creative enough to make their Halloween costumes?

As a child, it never dawned on me that Daddy worked long days, had other things to do, or would rather be reading the paper or relaxing for the evening. Kids never understand the sacrifices their parents make for them. Melanie, mother of four, once told me, "You never know how much your parents loved you until you have kids yourself."

She was right.

Daddy in His Derby Hat

12

WEED WAR

We have had such a mild winter up until this past week. I have
played tennis about twice a month at least outside. Everything was
in bloom and getting green, but as it usually does, this cold spell has
put it back. I had kale up but think it can probably take it. I got the
seeds when I took the "Miss Daisy's" to the Garden Show. Kale is
not my favorite thing, but it is pretty, and I like to see it grow. The
package said you could plant it in February, so I said, "why not?"
Place your orders early with me for your kale.
—Letter to Family, March 17, 1992

The suspects have been narrowed down to four men. The culprit may have been Randy Atcher or Cactus Brooks, who I watched early every morning on the Louisville-based "T-Bar-V Ranch Show." Possibly, it was Captain Kangaroo, himself. Maybe even the garden-loving Mr. Green Jeans could be blamed for my actions. But one of these four men motivated me to commit a sin.

My young brain was affected by avid daily television

watching. After all, the lyrics from the T Bar V Ranch song often gurgled out of my mouth:

"Brush your teeth each morning,
  Get lots of sleep at night.
  Mind your mom and daddy
  'Cause they know what is right.
  Lots of exercise each day
  And eat up all your food.
  Always wear a great big smile
  That makes you look so good.
  Be sure to look both left and right
  Before you cross the street.
  And be with us tomorrow at nine
  When it's T Bar V Ranch Time!"

Even at a young age, I sang with gusto like Maw-Maw.

An obedient child, I always did exactly what adults told me. Whether it was Randy, Cactus, The Captain, or Mr. Green Jeans didn't matter. When one of those male television mentors, through the magic of TV, urged me, an impressionable young kid, to do a good deed for my parents, I did what they said.

Such simple advice. Such honorable intentions.

What could possibly go wrong from following the friendly advice offered in 1960's children's television programming?

"I can do that," I said, smiling to myself early one summer day while dragging a hoe as tall as I was out of the garage. "They said to help with chores. Daddy will be so happy." Humming the "Whistle While You Work" song, (I had to hum it because I couldn't whistle) I strode bravely out over the moist, brown plot of dirt behind our hedgerow, ready to go to war with the wild things.

Scrawny-limbed, tow-headed, pre-grade-school me, began to whack away at the shaggy weeds in Daddy's flower bed with a fervor worthy of a warrior. The long handle of that hoe extended far behind my tiny body, circling and drooping, arcing and falling like a pterodactyl swooping for prey. I swung that hoe like a battle axe, hacking and chopping all those nasty opponents in the field. Holding my weapon up until my arms quivered, I'd then drop it furiously to the plant, instantly beheading it.

Until I was interrupted by the roar of a war whoop. Loud and insistent.

"Missi!" A deep voice was shouting my name just off the battlefield.

"Missi!" I heard it again.

Daddy came charging through the hedge, barreling toward me. "Missi! Go inside. *Now!"*

My hoe and I were dumbstruck. This man was yelling at me. Me. The girl who was just trying to help. Doing a good deed, just like the television guys told me to do.

"I mean it, Miss. Stop. Right this minute!" Daddy stepped closer, his voice louder than I'd ever heard it. His face looked like a red balloon about to pop.

"Drop that hoe now! Don't touch anything else!"

Tears blurred the bludgeoned plants below my conquering feet. My little knees began to shake. My warrior courage was gone, evaporating into the air with Daddy's shouts.

"Go to your room," Daddy roared. "Right this minute!"

"But, Daddy!" I wailed as he pointed dramatically to the house, extending his arm toward the back porch like an angry scarecrow.

"Go, now!"

Fear hit. I turned, dropping my hoe next to its slain victims. I had never heard Daddy roar before.

Beating a hasty retreat, I threw open the back door and ran through the house to my room, where I threw myself face-down on the blue-chenille bedspread. What had I done wrong? Why wasn't Daddy happy? Didn't he notice all the weeds I'd conquered? Couldn't he see the good deed I was doing? My head whirred with confusion.

That warm summer day the year I was six, after my morning television fix, I had single-handedly beheaded Daddy's entire flower crop with my hoe.

From that day forward, I couldn't see a Bachelor Button without my stomach clenching.

In my defense, Bachelor Buttons are scraggly-looking plants, and the ones Daddy had planted were not yet showing their fluffy, dandelion-like blue and pink flowers. Their blue-green floppy foliage did indeed look like weeds. (Even though any one over the age of six would surely have noticed that they were arranged in tidy rows and they were all of equal height.)

To Daddy's credit, he didn't cuss, throw things, or beat me. He never did. Under any circumstance. All things considered, he disciplined me in a typical Daddy fashion. He got over it and laughed about it later. After he spent some time working in the dirt, salvaging what plants he could while regaining his composure, he came to me in my blue and yellow bedroom. He sat down on the twin bed where I had hurtled myself face down, unaware of the imprint the chenille knots dots were making on my cheek. (My face looked like a pockmarked monkey.)

"Miss, I know you were just trying to help." I heard the resignation and frustration in his voice as he patted my back. "Next time, just ask me first."

I could have told him then that there would never be a "next time."

Over the following fifty years, I toured Daddy's gardens

hundreds of times, always with him as guide. I admired the red wax begonias planted in the narrow flower bed in front of the porch. I listened to his adventures in tomato planting. I watched as he pronounced the names of his rose bushes, waving his arm over each one while saying, "That's my Tiffany Rose. That's Queen Elizabeth." I bought Daddy plants, asked advice from his store of garden-lore, and shared my own landscaping ideas with him. I even laughed with him years later when he recounted the story of his tiny daughter "busting his blooms," and "deflowering his flora." But I never again tried to "help" with weeding on Driftwood Drive.

EASTER BANG-UP

"Why don't you get a haircut? You look like a chrysanthemum."
—W. P. Wodehouse

At eight, I was gawky and super-skinny with toothpick-like legs and a goofy ever-present grin. For some odd reason, I thought that to have my picture taken I had to loll my head to one side and smile sweetly. A camera-smile meant baring my top teeth and keeping my bottom lip tight —more a grimace than a grin. (Not my best look. Not *anyone's* best look.)

My sister, Melanie, five years older than me, was just coming into her own beauty. She had big, brown doe eyes, a golden tan, a slim build, and a smooth complexion with no zits. She was thirteen on that memorable Easter Sunday morning so it took her a long time to forgive Daddy for what he did. Even now, fifty years later, there's a spark of outrage when she talks about this episode of Johnson history.

Daddy was a can-do kind of guy. I'm not sure how or why

this came about, whether Mother and Daddy were short of money, whether they were short of time, whether Daddy just decided that he couldn't see enough of his girls' faces, or whether he just got this crazy "hare-brained" idea (excuse the pun), but he decided he was going to trim our bangs.

I have no idea where Mother was during this incident. Being totally unhandy, (in all her eighty-five years, I never saw her use a screwdriver or pick up a hammer,) she would have never dreamed of trying her hand at hair-trimming. She may have been loading the Easter baskets, carefully counting the number of jellybeans so that each daughter received exactly the same number of beans. Maybe she was shopping for those last-minute Easter accessories for our annually-purchased new spring outfits. (Once, Melanie and I had matching sister dresses of navy blue with white lace trim. Once, I had a new spring green coat. Every year, we each got a new dress, and sometimes a new pair of socks, a hat—when that was all the rage, or if the stars aligned, Mother would get us each a cute little purse to match our outfits.) If she had just hauled the ironing board out of our tiny kitchen closet to press those pastel cotton frocks for Sunrise Service the next morning, she could have put a stop to Daddy's subversive activities. But she did not.

I never questioned Daddy or even worried about the outcome. In my mind, Daddy could do anything. After all, I was a funky-looking kid whose bangs were never straight anyway because of crazy cowlicks that sprang like goat horns from either side of my forehead. Michele was even younger than I was, with rosy cheeks and dark ringlets dripping down around a cherubic face. My younger sister and I were always a team, and she was nonchalant as she lined up on the hearth. Being the youngest, she was always first, and I stood fidgeting next to her, waiting my turn.

After Michele hopped down, Daddy started on me. "Wait

a minute, Miss. Let me do that again." A second later he said, "I'm just going to even that up a little. Okay. Stand still." I'm sure it was beyond his skill level to account for the "lift-power" of those erratic cowlicks on each side of my forehead. After he was finished, I jumped down to follow Michele and didn't hang around to watch Daddy finish up with Melanie.

That year was the only year that all the Johnson women received corsages to wear on Easter morning. Boxes of white carnations trimmed with ribbons to match our Easter dresses arrived from Aebersold Florist that Saturday afternoon. To this day, I don't know if Daddy wanted to trim our bangs so we'd look good for the surprise he had planned or if the corsages were an unspoken apology for what he had done, a hope that some flashy flowers pinned to our chests would detract attention from our hair.

The picture in our family album tells all. Michele and I, young and giggly, stand on the fireplace sill. Michele's corsage stands out against her bright pink Easter dress. Her dark curls look none the worse for wear. I stand in my lavender-smocked affair, hands clasped in a saintly pose, bangs nearly absent on the right side of my forehead, but swooping down to a bristly, bush-like glob on my left.

But Melanie. Brand-new teenager, Melanie. Eyes red, wearing a forced smile, she sports auburn bangs sheared down to less than a half an inch, forming a bowl-like shape of tiny fringe around her forehead. Her grown-up outfit of a white blazer with a crest sewn on the pocket and a navy pleated plaid skirt can't overcome the hair disaster or hide the fact that she was furious with Daddy. (She had every right to be!) No corsage in the world, no matter how color-ful, how large, or how fragrant, could divert attention from Daddy's handiwork. His foray into hair design proved that he would never be a barber, much less a stylist, and his 'can-do' attitude with regard to our grooming disappeared from that day forward.

Daddy never again took up a pair of scissors against us, but for years afterward he joked about it. He laughed loudly at the story, throwing his hands up in the air as he described Melanie's hair. She may, all these decades later, sport just the hint of a smile at the reminiscence as Daddy would talk about the year he perpetrated the "Easter Bang-Up."

Easter Bang-Up

14

WALKING ON THE WILD SIDE

"Whoever is not in his coffin and the dark grave, let him know he has enough."
—Walt Whitman

I f it weren't for Daddy, the Johnson girls would never have experienced the natural world at all. Mother was all about working, faithfully performing her duties as a nurse for an allergist for more than thirty years. Mother's natural habitat was a retail store, where she could prowl forever. Shopping, reading, and writing were the things she loved to do. All most definitely "inside" hobbies. Not one thing pulled her out-of-doors. Gardening, walking outside, fishing, swimming, or just sitting on the porch would never cross her mind. Daddy, on the other hand, was a creature of the wild.

Somehow, without us even recognizing the magic he was bestowing, he imbued his love of nature to his three daughters. The simple pleasure he took in nature showed in the things he taught us, like how to make the bloom of a snapdragon "snap" by pressing on either side of the flower. Or by showing us how to suck the "honey" out of the honeysuckle. Or by making grass "cry" by picking a long piece, holding it between both thumbs with hands cupped around it, and blowing on it. Sometimes he'd tell us to look for four-leaf clovers, and we'd sit in the grass forever, usually picking plain old ordinary three-leaf-clovers and then tying them into chains to wear around our neck.

We would all come running when Daddy said, "Let's take a walk in the woods."

Our house on Driftwood Drive was one of the first ones in what was the "new" section of Blackiston Heights. Behind our newly constructed home was nothing but open fields, a falling-down storage building, and the thick woods that bordered the edge of the subdivision. Six years old when we moved into that house, I would have never ventured into the darkened frontier of the woods without Daddy, but after a few hikes with him, I knew to follow the dirt path until it made a right turn into the woods.

One spring day shortly after we settled in, Daddy took us on our first walk on the wild side. He led the way, followed by Melanie, then me, then Michele, trailing him like he was our own Pied Piper. Chattering, jumping, skipping, we crossed from the path at the edge of the field into the dark woods. Instantly, we grew quieter, the trees shivering and shaking as if they had absorbed our noisy energy. Three trusting, silent girls followed Daddy deeper into the woods, walking a narrow path trodden only by deer. Daddy must have known where he was going from his boyhood treks through the hills and hollows of southern Indiana because he led us straight to a sight that made me suck in my breath.

Bright daffodils sprang up from the leaf-covered ground, spewing color into the dim light. A bunch here. A bunch there. Some were white jonquils, their cups outlined in a deep shade of red. Others were hot yellow with curly petals. Several clumps were a combination of orange and lemon, like blossoms painted with sunlight.

"A secret garden!" I gasped with pleasure. Then my eyes focused on what was in shadow behind the flowers. Something that stopped me in my tracks. Something that made my stomach flip.

Sitting at odd angles, camouflaged by daffodils, were dozens of tombstones.

Daddy had taken us to a forgotten cemetery, an old graveyard originally on some settler's land or occupied by the residents of some long-ago farmstead. Obviously untended and unvisited, the cemetery was beautiful, quiet, and only a little spooky.

What do you know about grave markers at the age of seven? Not much. But I could tell they were old, special in a way I couldn't explain. Spattered with dusty white spots, etched over with moss, the stones looked like guards leaning over souls they'd been planted to protect.

Daddy ambled over the damp ground, browsing the names and dates on the headstones, many of them dating back to the 1800's. "Imagine, girls, the stories these graves could tell if they could talk," Daddy mused as he waved his arm over the plots. Any waft of eeriness dissipated into the shadows as we made up stories about the names on the graves, bending to pick daffodils as he did so. Stories emerged as each sister contributed a quote, a detail, or a plot twist.

For years, in a ritualistic springtime adventure, Daddy and his daughters went to pick daffodils in our "secret garden" in the woods.

Turns out it was not so secret after all.

One year, Melanie came home from high school, chattering with great excitement about how the police had come to school that afternoon and arrested two students. She had watched the drama from her classroom window. The "criminals" had worn old jewelry to the cafeteria and flashed garnet, onyx, and pearl rings on greedy, waving fingers. The guy pulled a skull from the pocket of his pea coat, rubbing its head to elicit screams from the girls around him.

Apparently, we were not the only neighborhood kids to wander down the paths and stumble on the old cemetery. Not everyone appreciated the beauty and sanctity of the place. The two teenagers Melanie talked about had skipped school to brazenly dig up the graves in our secret garden.

Several times after the grave-robbing escapade, Daddy and his girls went back. In junior high, Michele and I would go back by ourselves to pick daffodils and to feel like brave adventurers hiking into dangerous territory, but the woods were never the same. Gaping holes in the black ground looked like the vacant eyes of a skeleton. Smashed headstones lying helter-skelter amidst the dead defied the sense of peace. The mystical quality was gone, killed by some crazy kids who would ghoulishly dig up coffins and steal from dead people.

The grave-robbery was my first inkling that people were not always nice, that the world was scary outside of Blackiston Heights, and that not even Daddy could keep evil away.

15

THE VIOLATION OF MOLLY MALONE

"The robb'd that smiles steals something from the thief..."
—William Shakespeare, Othello

B eing the first house on a street in a new neighborhood meant that we had no neighbors close by. We existed with the back of our house to the fields and the side to the woods. Our street was short, not yet developed into the compacted middle-class neighborhood it would become.

It was quiet and isolated.

That is why one evening our long black Chevy pulled up the hill to our little brick house on Driftwood Drive to find a nasty surprise.

Mother and Daddy had assigned their daughters very specific jobs. We were always responsible for jumping out of the car and running up the slope to open the garage door. (As a parent, I now understand that assigning kids the jobs that require legwork and physical exertion is a good strategy.) The job always defaulted to Melanie who was bigger, stronger, and smarter than her twittering little sisters. She was also more "grown-up" and in a hurry to escape a back-seat with the two annoying twitter-ers. That summer evening, as soon as the car paused on the driveway hill, Melanie jumped out of the back seat, jogged up the slope, leaned over, and heaved upward on the metal pull of the noisy garage door. (It's come to my attention that it was actually a guy named Mr. Johnson who invented the automatic door opener in 1926. No relation. While the devices were becoming popular in the mid-sixties, this Johnson family did not have one. We were technology-challenged and slow to grab new gadgets, so we wouldn't have a garage door opener for at least another decade. Mother and Daddy chose to utilize the muscle power of their sturdy-legged daughters instead.)

After performing her door-duty, Melanie strutted through the garage, opened the interior door to the family room, took a few steps into the kitchen and stopped short.

The back door was standing wide open.

By this time the rest of us had come in, jamming like Pick-Up sticks into the small area behind the kitchen door.

"Melanie, are you okay?" Daddy asked.

"It was just standing there, wide open!" Melanie gasped out.

"Are you okay?" Daddy asked again.

It had only been a minute since she'd come in. "What could have possibly happened to her anyway?" I thought, trying to process Daddy's question through the filter of an eight-year-old brain.

Daddy's voice cut through my confusion. I stood looking, but not grasping what had happened.

"Melanie. Are you okay? What did you see?" Daddy demanded again.

Her eyes as big as black holes, Melanie repeated, "The door was wide open!"

(So were her eyes.)

Daddy kept asking questions. "Did you see anything? Hear anything when you came in?"

"No!" Melanie gulped. "I just saw the back door was WIDE OPEN!"

"Wide open" must have had some special significance to her because she kept saying that. LOUDLY.

"Don't worry," Daddy said. "It's okay. I'll just check the house to make sure there's no one here."

He was so brave, marching out the kitchen and down the hallway, turning on lights and peering into each of the three bedrooms.

Mother and daughters held their breath while Daddy searched the house. Whether we were prepared to run outside screaming or pull salad forks out of the silverware drawer and attack if an invader materialized, I have no clue.

"Well, we must have surprised some burglars, but it doesn't look like they got very much," Daddy reassured us. "Probably just a couple of kids. When we pulled in, they saw the lights and ran back through the field." Daddy wasn't rattled.

We were. Michele and I grabbed hands, holding onto each other for courage as we tiptoed down the hall into our bedroom. At the time, the walk down that short hallway seemed miles long. Our hearts pounded with excitement and anticipation. For some obscure reason, we felt the need to be quiet, sneaking into our room as if we were the prowler. The chiffon-yellow bedroom we shared was filled with twin beds, one dresser, and a nightstand. On each of our beds was a broken piggy bank.

"Oh, no! They broke my bank! Molly Malone is DEAD!" I wailed.

My mother, proud of her Irish heritage and her name, "Molly," had told us about Molly Malone many times. Though Mother was totally incapable of producing music, she would sometimes hum a weak, off-kilter tune:

"In Dublin's fair city
  Where the girls are so pretty
  I first set my eyes on sweet Molly Malone
  As she wheeled her wheelbarrow
  Through the streets broad and narrow
  Crying "cockles and mussels, alive, alive, oh"
  "Alive, alive, oh"
  "Alive, alive, oh"
  Crying "cockles and mussels, alive, alive, oh."

Somewhere along the way, Mother had gifted me with a bank depicting an Irish girl selling her baskets of fish. Now, poor Molly's body had been violently broken. Her red-haired skull lay, decapitated, on my pillow among shards of bright plaster and lifeless fish-eyes.

Moher and Daddy were there to calm us. "Oh, it's just a bank," Daddy said. "The important thing is that we're all okay. Whoever did this ran out the door when they saw the lights of the car coming up the driveway. They couldn't have been here long, and they certainly didn't take much."

"But it's *not* just a bank," I moaned.

"We can get a new one," Mother reassured me. She knew about the connection of emotion to things and the thrill of possessing cool items. Besides, she was the ultimate shopper, comforting me with the promise that we could get just go to the store and get another bank.

"But it's my Molly Malone bank!" I whined as I noticed just a few nickels and pennies scattered on the blue chenille bedspread beneath bits of broken plaster.

"And they took my silver dollars from Paw-Paw!"

Paw-Paw was Daddy's father who had died when I was just five. I had few memories of him except that he loved candy, particularly Brach's orange slices and lemon drops, always had Kool-Aid around, and that he gave each of his three granddaughters a couple of silver dollars.

Filled with hot anguish, I bawled, gulping air in quick breaths. "And they took my 'UGLY'" prize money! NOOOOO! They can't have my Kennedy dollar!" Anger had quickly replaced any fear. I had, after all, won that money because I, alone, was the ugliest costumed-kid in the McClure's parking lot that Halloween, a proud moment in my young life.

I was outraged by the loss of my funds and the invasion of my space. It was MY bank, MY money, MY room! (Perhaps it was a sign that I was valuing the wrong thing at this early point in my life. That wealth was more important than safety? That possessions were the ultimate in the life of an eight-year-old? Maybe a normal reaction to being robbed, no matter your age, is just to get plain mad. I was fuming.)

Even though Mother and Daddy must have had some kind of emotional reaction to the burglary, they appeared calm and rational to us, accepting what had happened and going on without drama. No hysteria. No fear. No anger. They must have talked about the robbery to each other, but nothing was ever said to us. Their reaction was an example of how to be calm in the face of danger. (Okay. It wasn't really dangerous since the burglars were probably kids who went after piggy banks first instead of stereos or tools. But still...)

Daddy talked to the police while we swept up our broken childhood baubles. Television, appliances, and jewelry were accounted for. Mother and Daddy opened the garage door themselves for a day or two, before the job defaulted back to

Melanie. Eventually, we all stopped checking to see if the back door was open every time we came in the house. Life got back to normal.

Somehow, somewhere, sometime shortly after our home invasion, Mother worked a shopping miracle. She found another Molly Malone bank for me. (What are the odds of *that*? Was Molly Malone a trending figure in the mid 1960's? How in a world before online shopping, had Mother secured a second Molly Malone bank? How many hours did she search for that? Did I ever thank her for that amazing feat?) The new Molly was blonde, wore a bright turquoise rain slicker, flaunted a neon-orange rain hat, and clenched a bundle of fish in her hands. This "Molly" survived and lived a good long life, now residing with my own granddaughter, Faith, where, hopefully, she will never be broken to bits, vandalized, and violated.

While the sanctity of our home and the honor of Molly Malone had been violated, it was a temporary setback. The Bum's Corner was still an idyllic place to live and remained that way for the next fifty-five years, a shining spot in a happy childhood.

16

SPINE-TINGLING STORIES OUT OF LEFT FIELD

"Now in later years, your father became a great story-teller. He would start going off on this and that, and he'd keep talking about something, and Bill and I used to just enjoy listening. Your Dad would keep us entertained. I think all his stories were true, but they were just things you never heard about, and he could make them sound good. He loved telling stories. He was great at that."
—Father Pete Interview, April 2018

The old gray Nova dawdled along. Daddy was running errands, me in tow, adding a little sightseeing to the day. Driving around the first mud road in the next planned section of Blackiston Heights, an area at the very bottom of Johnson Lane, Daddy stopped the car and told me a story.

"I think this is where it happened, Miss. Somewhere around in here."

"What happened, Daddy?"

"My great Uncle Joe, when he was a kid, lost a dog here."

"What do you mean, 'lost?' Like he ran away and was lost?"

"No. Like his dog was lost forever…killed here."

"Killed? By a car?" The words were slow because I ten and overly emotional, saddened by the idea of a boy losing his dog.

"No. Cars weren't around then. This was in the 1870's. Remember, he was my grandmother's brother, so it was a long time ago."

I nodded, wide-eyed. My Maw-Maw was ancient. It was impossible to imagine how old Daddy's grandmother and her brother would have been, or what it was like when they walked around this field.

"Uncle Joe was going through this field with his dog when he looked up and saw a terrible sight. A couple of wolves were loping towards him." Daddy pointed straight ahead to the open field in front of the car.

"Wolves? Real wolves? We don't have those around here, Daddy," I argued.

"Not now, we don't, Miss, but this was almost a hundred years ago. There weren't houses around here and not a lot of people lived here yet."

I kept listening. Daddy knew a lot about history, so I guessed he was right.

"Uncle Joe ran to the edge of the field to a tree line, and he climbed up. His dog ran with him and stayed at the base of the tree. Uncle Joe had to sit up in that tree and look down while those two wolves tore his dog to pieces

My eyes widened.

"I always liked Uncle Joe," Daddy continued, as if he hadn't just told me a horror story that could give me nightmares for months.

The gory scene glowed red in my head. How horrible

would it be to watch Moses the cat torn to shreds by wolves and not be able to do anything about it.

Daddy was in full storytelling mode now, just warming up.

Squinting as he gazed across the field that would soon be surrounded by houses, Daddy went on without looking at me. "Once, when I was a young boy, my parents and I went to visit my great Uncle Joe on a Sunday afternoon. We walked into the barn where his current Shepherd-Collie dog had a litter of pups."

I felt a little better knowing Uncle Joe hadn't given up entirely on dogs after his own traumatic experience as a boy.

"Well, Uncle Joe was a big, handsome guy who lived on a farm. He looked me in the eye and asked me right out, 'Would you like to have a puppy, Melford?'" Daddy looked at me as he laughed. "What boy doesn't want a puppy?"

I smiled and nodded, grateful this wasn't a scary story.

"My Dad told me it was okay. 'Pick One,' he said, and out of that litter I chose a good-looking pup I called 'Shep.' I was very fond of that dog."

If I asked Daddy what had ever happened to Shep, I don't remember, but I could safely assume that Shep had not fallen prey to the wolves like his predecessor.

Having Daddy tell me things like this, just talking to me as I sat on the passenger seat and surveyed the same field he watched, was exhilarating. I was in my own private story-time with him, thinking that I was the "special" daughter, the one worthy of receiving the family stories. The best thing about it, though, is that the things Daddy was telling me were true, not made-up book stuff.

"I remember a couple of other stories about Uncle Joe," Daddy said. "My Mother told about the time that Uncle Joe rode his horse down to my Grandmother's house. Your Maw-

Maw would have been about your age, and she remembered it vividly. She said Uncle Joe rode up to the front of the house and yelled for them to come out. He didn't even get off the horse, but he shouted out to the family, "Whatever you do, don't come over home. Stay away. Three of the kids are dead of diphtheria."

"Oh, no!" I shook my head in dismay. "What's diphtheria? It sounds horrible."

Daddy patiently explained, moving his hands up and down his neck, rubbing his glands to show me. "Diphtheria is a sickness that causes your throat to swell up so that you can't breathe. The air passages are blocked. Basically, people just suffocate. Now we have vaccines for it, but it used to kill lots of people."

"Yuk. That sounds awful," I groaned.

"Yes, it must have been awful," Daddy admitted. I can't imagine seeing three of your children die within ten days. But that's not the most awful story," he said. "Your Maw-Maw told me another one."

No way. First wolves eating dogs. Then kids dying from horrible diseases. What could be worse than *that*?

"Well, Miss," Daddy started in again in dramatic form. "Uncle Joe had ten kids. The oldest was Albert. Albert committed suicide by slitting his own throat."

I sucked in air and leaned back in the seat, trying to escape the horror of it all.

Daddy didn't notice my distress.

"Uncle Joe and my grandmother lived close together, and things weren't any different than they are now. When tragedy strikes one family member, the others rush in to help, so my grandmother and her kids were at Uncle Joe's, helping however they could. Just being there, comforting their cousins, cooking, baking, and setting up for the wake in their parlor." Daddy kept talking, even though I was a little freaked out.

"According to my Mother, she was curious. Later she said she didn't know what in the world would possess her to do it, but before they removed Albert's body, when no one was looking, she lifted the sheet off his stiff, dead corpse to get a look."

In later years, I, too, heard Maw-Maw tell this story. She may not have used as much inflection and gesturing as Daddy did when he told it, but the horror in her wrinkled old face was real. "Well, I never to this day know what caused me to do it. It was an *awful* sight!" Maw-Maw shook her head at her own stupidity and morbid curiosity.

Why would Daddy tell me such scary stories?

Maybe when a tale is told under the guise of family history, no matter how creepy, Daddy thought it was acceptable. Like classic ghost stories, the tales Daddy told fascinated and frightened me at the same time. While I may not have had nightmares, those Uncle Joe stories lived on in me a long, long, long time after Uncle Joe.

17

MAN AND THE MOON MUSIC

"Also bought the sheet music for Clair de Lune, *simplified version. I've been working on it, and I think that maybe before I lose my hearing and sight, I may be able to play it. I certainly enjoy trying. Mother and I are working on it together."*
—Letter to Molly, May 24, 1952

T he man flickering on the screen in the old home movie is movie star good-looking. Slim. Young. Strong jawed. Hair so dark it glitters in the light.

A round-faced, curly-headed girl sits on the bench next to him, bounced upward by the rhythm of the two chubby legs she's throwing back against the piano bench. One taller, dark-complexioned girl stands to one side of the bench, left hand touching the keyboard. A short, blonde girl, head cocked to one side, completes the picture.

Mouths open wide like ventriloquist dummies as the narrow old film clicks and clatters unevenly through the machine. The man's hands flicker over the keyboard, his movements reflected back into the camera by the mirror behind the piano.

No sound comes from the old movie, but music pours forth anyway.

One instance captured in time. Thousands of instances in real life.

Daddy taught us to sing by example, not instruction. He just sat down at the piano, played whatever came to mind, and we were pulled like magnets to the sound.

He unknowingly gave concerts on Sunday mornings. While we'd be getting ready, or before we'd even gotten up, Daddy would have dressed, made dinner for after church, walked around the yard, and retrieved the paper. While he was waiting for his "harem," he'd sit down at the piano and play. Always, always, we'd have to wait for Mother, who was never once ready early. Even when she walked down the short hall into the living room, she'd spend time checking to make sure the back door was locked, the lights were off. Just when it seemed like there was nothing else to do, she'd gasp, "Oh, darn! I forgot my handkerchief/purse/keys/book." Mother would rush off to retrieve whatever it was that she needed, leaving us more music time around the piano with Daddy.

The tune we all cut our teeth on was "Moon, Moon." Daddy's favorite one had us crooning and scooping notes, pulling out a syncopated rhythm with real attitude:

"Moon, Moon, great big silvery moon,
   Won't you please shine down on me?
   Moon, Moon, great big silvery moon,
   Hidin' behind that tree.
   There stands a man with a big shot gun,
   Ready to shoot ya' if you start to run,
   So Moon, Moon, great big silvery moon."

You may be asking, 'What father would sing to his young daughters about men lying in wait armed with a shotgun just waiting to pull the trigger?' Mel Johnson would. To Daddy, it was just an old song with backwoods lyrics. To us, it was the melody that taught us how to sing together, just a fun ditty that we would sing from the time we learned to talk until the time we can no longer talk at all. (Researching the lyrics later, I found out that this is a song called "Mr. Moon," an old Midwest camp song with no traceable links to author or origination. Different versions of the words exist, although they are all very similar. Daddy sang the Kansas version.)

Let me be clear. Daddy was *not* a polished musician. He didn't have a great voice. His playing and singing were loose and imperfect. He would never win any awards for his voice or his keyboard skills. All the same, nothing brought us more happiness than hearing him play or singing by his side. Music was a gift of joy he shared.

For decades, Centenary Church Choir benefitted from his happy-go-lucky singing, a light-volume tenor in every hymn. Daddy went to practice on Wednesday nights and sang in the choir loft on Sunday mornings. Never a leader or soloist, he raised his voice to strengthen the group. He knew the words to dozens of hymns and smiled when he sang them. Truth be told, he was glad to be in the tenor section because of the seating configuration. The tenors were happily hidden by the altar cloth from view of the congregation. Comfortably settled there, Daddy found he didn't have to fight the urge to doze. Ask anyone in the Centenary crowd if they'd ever seen Daddy snoozing during the sermon and they'd say "yes" since to say otherwise would mean that lightning would strike them dead.

One Sunday, it sounded like lightning had struck.

Daddy, singing in the tenor section, conveniently secreted

behind the altar and out of sight, fell asleep, head against the wall.

Boom. Ka-plunk.

The entire congregation startled, but not as much as Daddy.

The panel in the wall behind Daddy's head had given way, violently ending Daddy's nap and ensnaring his head in the dark cavity. He carefully pulled his head out of the narrow space and stood up, bowing, laughing, and waving to the minister, mid-sermon, and to the grinning assembly of worshippers.

Some of Daddy's musical flair took hold in Melanie, who began taking piano lessons at a young age. Whether talent is genetic, or whether it's passed through some kind of ancestral osmosis, I don't know, but Melanie got more of it than Michele and I did. She became a talented pianist, accompanist for the Clarksville High School Concert Choir, mentored and guided by the beautiful, demanding-your-best Lynn Lewis. Melanie earned her spending money with part-time gigs. She played piano for the early service at church and was often sought out as accompanist at special events like weddings, parties, and funerals.

What you can learn from listening to music! Michele and I absorbed classical music, choral harmony, and musical vocabulary from hearing Melanie play. The big mirror above the piano would see her wrinkling her forehead, marking a passage, or clapping out a rhythm. She spent hours perfecting pieces that the Concert Choir would sing. The best thing about Melanie's role in the high school music department was that she would often have section rehearsals at our house. At some specified time, a group of good-looking guys from the bass section would appear on our front porch and be ushered in to stand around the piano. I would listen breathlessly to the music they made and watch them, awestruck, in the mirror. Their rehearsals were punctuated with funny comments and good-natured teasing.

Sometimes, two sections would come at the same time, creating harmonies that would vibrate my bones. Altos and tenors. Sopranos and altos. Tenors and basses. Each combination made my mind buzz.

Because I had a bit of the vocal gene, when I was in seventh grade, Melanie asked me to come sing with a section rehearsal. They were working on a piece about the Civil War called "One Wore Blue and One Wore Gray." My thready soprano intermingled with the big boys' booming vocals that day, and I was transported to my own musical paradise.

All three Johnson girls loved music, and we each had our own strength. Michele had the gift of grace. Her ability to hear melody and rhythm led her to be a dancer. The entire family was proud when Michele auditioned and won a spot as a "Red-Stepper" for Indiana University. She kicked and strutted, marched and pinwheeled, in those high-heeled red boots. Even now, she can really "cut a rug" at family weddings.

As a "gift" to Daddy on his seventy-fifth birthday, Lynn Lewis, then choir director at Centenary Methodist Church, asked "The Johnson Girls" to sing at the Sunday service. Dutifully, we practiced and performed "Let There Be Peace On Earth," a piece we had all performed at church and at school. Both Mother and Daddy loved the song and had been moved when the Concert Choir had sung it at each daughter's spring concert, right before graduation.

Performing for Daddy in our old home church under the watchful eye of Lynn, we became nervous and timid. The Johnson girls sang more like young kids, shyly mouthing Sunday school songs than mature women offering a vocal tribute of love. Singing to a sanctuary full of people who had known us from birth was different than singing around the piano at home on Driftwood Drive. What was it about being an adult in your childhood church that made you feel you weren't worthy? We were all professional women, but we were not professional vocalists, and we all had that "A" type personality that decreed if we weren't doing it perfectly, we shouldn't do it at all. Self-consciously, worried that we would disappoint our beloved Mrs. Lewis, and aware that nothing we could sing would ever be enough of a tribute to Daddy, we got through it. It wasn't bad, but it wasn't memorable, either.

But Daddy thought we were amazing. We could have sung the violence-laden "Moon, Moon, Great Big Silvery Moon" to the church audience and he would have thought we were worthy of Carnegie Hall.

His pride knew no bounds even though our talent did.

Daddy's musical talent was not exceptional. But it was boundless. Effortless. Joyful. He whistled when he worked. He danced with us in the kitchen. He played and sang and hummed, and even when he wasn't doing it out loud, the melodies floated inside him. The songs didn't flow from his fingers. The music didn't come from his vocal chords. It poured forth from his soul.

18

YULE BE SORRY

*"I just got Molly off to work. It is a cool, rainy morning. We had a
fire in the fireplace last night, and it was still burning this
morning. She said I was cruel as I sat in front of the fire reading
my newspaper, drinking coffee, and watching the news on TV as
she went out the door to face the cold, cold world. Some guys just
have it all though!"*
—Letter to Missi, April 24, 1995

Daddy was a self-proclaimed "River Rat." Having
grown-up on the banks of the Ohio, he fished, swam,
and played in it his entire life. One of his favorite pastimes,
well through his seventies, was walking along the banks,
picking up driftwood, and finding firewood that he would
haul home in the trunk of his car. He was proud of collecting
"free" fuel and would gleefully throw it in the fireplace
through the cold winter months. Each year, Daddy would
make it his goal to find the biggest, driest, hardest piece of
wood he could find on the riverbanks to use on Christmas

Eve. It was a Johnson tradition that once the Yule log was put on the fire, it had to burn throughout the night and still be glowing Christmas morning when the second-to-largest log would be thrown on.

The Christmas of 1970, when I was twelve, Mother had been cooking all day for company. My grandparents, Maw-Maw, and Nanny and Baw-Baw were coming for Christmas Eve dinner. Mother had moved the maple, drop-leaf table out into the living room so we'd have room for more people than could fit in the cramped alcove in the kitchen. She had set the table with her gold-edged, ivory china with blue wheat stalks swaying in the middle of each plate. Her traditional roast and browned potatoes, (always cooked dry and nearly lifeless,) sat in the oven, while her fancy cranberry Jell-O mold congealed in the freezer. The "stockings were hung by the chimney with care," the tree lights sparkling, and we were ready to celebrate Christmas Eve.

Daddy decided it was time to put his traditional Yule log on the fire—one he was particularly proud of this year because of its immense size. It was all he could do to lift it, staggering up the one step of the garage where the firewood was kept and heaving it in, huffing ragged breaths.

It wasn't more than a minute before giant clouds of dense gray smoke were rolling out of the tiny family room and into the kitchen, billowing down the narrow hallway, into the living room and every inch of that brick home on Driftwood Drive. Mother frantically threw open the doors and started flapping her dish towel like a manic, but inept, bullfighter.

Daddy was shouting, "The flue is jammed! The flue is jammed!" Lesser men would have been shouting profanities and throwing cuss words, but in all my life, I never heard Daddy curse. Not once. Even though smoke was flowing fast and furious, Daddy somehow got that hot log out of the fireplace by himself and unstuck the fireplace damper. The log went back in, and the rest of us rushed around waving rags, opening windows, spraying air freshener, and trying to "de-smoke" the house as all three of my grandparents arrived and were walking up the sidewalk.

It's a miracle that Daddy didn't blister his hands and that he was able to fix the problem without the house burning to ashes around us. Not everything was unscathed, though. All those Christmas stockings hung with such care were scorched black on their backsides. Some actually seeped chocolate from treats that had melted inside them. The house smelled like a campfire for weeks.

With his typical good humor and his joy at being a punster, Daddy joked for years about the "smoked" turkey we might have had, the "hot" chocolate served in stockings, and the infamous "Yule Be Sorry" Christmas Log.

19

SNAP, CRACKLE, POP

"I was also over to Virg and Edna's. Edna was describing all the excitement that she was in today. A garage at the end of the lane caught fire, and Edna and one of the neighbor ladies were the first to arrive. The antics Edna goes through describing what happened are hilarious.

It was a big garage, very near the house, which came very near catching fire also. Edna helped some man get a small garden tractor out before several gas cans exploded. She then broke the kitchen door and got into the house to close the doors to avoid a draft, then helped throw water on the house until the fire engine came.

She said there was a large woman there who told her not to worry, that she had prayed and that the Lord had assured her the house would not catch on fire.

Edna said she told the lady she believed in prayer, but that she also thought a little water would help."
—Letter to Molly, April 29, 1952

"Snap!" A loud, cracking sound cut through the cold. Uncle Virg came skating toward us, fast and ferocious, like a cheetah on blades. His face was stubbled with beard and his glasses were thick, but his eyes were flashing.

Michele and I were dumbfounded, unable to comprehend what had just happened. Daddy might be sprawled on the ice between us now, but we had just been skating on either side of him, our arms linked through his.

Uncle Virg yelled as he skated across the pond. "Girls! Get to the house right now! Tell your aunt that your dad just broke his leg."

"What was he talking about?" I wondered. "What did he mean…Daddy just broke his leg?"

Just a few minutes ago, Daddy and Uncle Virg had been acting like kids, playing crack-the-whip with my teenaged cousins. These two old men, (at least they seemed old to the seventh-grade me,) had been laughing and hooting the whole time. Ice skating was as natural to Daddy and his brother as giggling was to me and my sister. Michele and I had been mesmerized, watching Daddy show off the spread eagles he learned as a kid. It must have taken hundreds of hours of skating on cold, country ponds to get that good. First, he would work up to a good speed, then point his toes outward, spread his arms straight out, lock his knees and lean, face forward, toward the ice. Suddenly, we understood why the trick was called a "Spread Eagle." Daddy looped around the pond in graceful majesty, floating across the gray ice without moving his legs. It was as if a wind eddy pushed him in circles over the frozen surface.

Inspired by his example, Michele and I had whooped in near delirium as we skated around the pond pretending to be

Olympic skaters. The new white skates Daddy had just bought me at K-Mart contained more magic than Dorothy's ruby red slippers, and they would surely make me a fabulous figure skater. Michele and I, always partners, jumped, went backwards, and worked on turning corners by crossing one foot over the other. Too full of ourselves to know we couldn't really do any of the fancy moves we thought we were doing, we were exhilarated, enthusiastic, and oh-so-cocky. We were, after all, Daddy's girls. Skating was in our blood.

So how had Daddy ended up sitting on the ice, a daughter on either side, like two gaping gargoyles guarding their master?

"Girls!" Uncle Virg was close to us now, shouting to get our attention. "Do you hear me? I mean it! Go tell your aunt I'm taking your dad to the hospital. He just broke his leg!"

I couldn't figure out how Uncle Virg *knew* daddy had broken his leg. He hadn't even gotten to him yet.

"Girls! *NOW!* Tell Edna what happened! Hurry."

Finally getting the point, Michele and I abandoned Daddy to Uncle Virg's care and turned and scrambled up the banks of the pond. We weaved and wobbled our way across the yard as fast as we could go on the single metal blades of our skates, yelling, "Aunt Edna! Aunt Edna!" the whole time.

Somehow, while we were running for the house, Uncle Virg, or maybe my older cousin Henry, got a pickup truck close enough to the pond that they could carry Daddy up the bank. We weren't there to hear Daddy moan or to see Uncle Virg and the boys haul Daddy into the truck and drive him to the hospital. We were busy with funny, plump, Aunt Edna.

Aunt Edna was jolly. No other word for it. Dark-haired, ruddy complexion, sparkling eyes. She smiled a lot, cracked jokes, and "shook like a bowl full of jelly" when she laughed, which was often. What happened after she ushered these two screaming, breathless girls into the house, I don't exactly remember. It took her awhile to get the story straight, because Michele and I were gasping out phrases, not coherent sentences.

"Daddy..." I huffed.

"Uncle Virg..." Michele puffed.

"B-B-Broke his leg..." I sputtered.

"...said to tell you!" Michele grunted.

"Now, now, girls. Take a breath." Aunt Edna patted each one of us on our chapped, rosy cheeks. "Breath deep. Go slow. Tell me," she said, her bright-pink, bow-like smile never faltering, "which one broke a leg?"

"Daddy!" Michele and I squealed in unison.

Somehow, Aunt Edna pieced together the story and went into action doing whatever it is that grown-ups do when someone breaks a leg on a frozen winter pond. Then she somehow made our terror go away. Part of her comfort involved placing big stoneware mugs of piping hot chocolate into our freezing hands. When she dropped in two tiny marshmallows, which floated around our cups looking like two tiny skaters on a pond, Aunt Edna's magic comfort got even sweeter.

Aunt Edna soothed us, but guilt assaulted me. I remember looking down and seeing a small twig right in Daddy's path as we were cruising across the ice. I didn't even warn him. Who knew that a twig, a tiny little stick laying on the ice, could wreak such havoc? The real cause of the accident wasn't just the stick, though. It was his very own daughters.

With one of us linked to him on each side, Daddy had no free hands. When he tripped, he knew that if he fell forward, Michele and I would go forward, too, bashing our faces, busting our elbows, nailing our knees. When his blade hit that twig, his momentum was stopped like stubbing a toe while running twenty miles per hour. Daddy sacrificed himself to save us. He dropped directly downward, not forward or backward, straight down on his leg. With all his body weight on top of him and the rock-hard ice below him, his leg had no choice but to shatter.

Michele and I stayed at Aunt Edna and Uncle Virg's house until Mother came to get us after getting Daddy settled in the hospital. He had broken his leg in six places, and the surgeons had put pins in to make it heal straight.

After a long winter of heavy casts, no driving, pain, and rehab, Daddy's broken leg healed. He declared he was "good as new," but Michele and I were still a little traumatized. We worried ourselves sick on the first night he was able to drive after those long weeks when he was chauffeured everywhere by Mother. That first night of doctor-sanctioned-driving, Daddy took Mother to their Sunday School party while Michele and I watched a particularly sad episode of *The Waltons*. We were sure that Daddy and Mother would be in some terrible accident on the way home, just like the sad ending to John-Boy's saga, and just after Daddy finally got well again. (Oh, the drama of pre-pubescent girls!)

Daddy had said that all women should know how to do three things: swim, type, and drive. But he gave us a bonus lesson when he showed us the joy of ice skating. Throughout my life, despite the breakage of bones at Uncle Virg's farm, ice skating has put me in a state of rapture.

Several years before Daddy broke his leg, he took us to Aunt Edna and Uncle Virg's for an evening outing. Six years old, I was surrounded by noisy shouts, nothing visible except orange sparks against the smoky blackness. The noise of metal scratching the surface of the pond was unmistakable. I was cold, but thoroughly enchanted.

Several years after Daddy broke his leg, when I was in high school, I skated around the local ice rink with a boy named Wayne. Wearing my cranberry ribbed turtleneck, a pair of bell bottom jeans that tied at the waist, and a cranberry and white checked jacket, I was sure I would enchant him with my grace and beauty on the ice. Compared to him, waving his big arms wildly to keep his balance, his ankles leaning inward like bent nails, I did look elegant. When he nicknamed me "Tiny Dancer," after the Elton John song, I was charmed. (Not nearly so charmed when I learned he had gone out with my close friend, Debbie that very same week and nicknamed her "Tiny Dancer," too!)

Decades later, after finding that I am a horrible skier, (it doesn't take much convincing when you land face down over a fence—on the bunny hill, no less— and you hear people all around you yelling, "Call an ambulance!") I tucked my tail between my legs in shame and headed for the skating rink at Breckinridge, Colorado. There, I watched as snow floated down in giant flakes and emerald pines dripped white lace from the mountains that surrounded me. Reassured by my old skates, tight-fitting and worn, but still serviceable, I circled the ice, glad that I wasn't terrible at everything. Satisfaction came, not in death-defying speed and downhill descents, but in the quiet grace of feet flirting with ice.

That crisp, distinctive "snap" heard that long ago day cracked through my consciousness twice more in my life. First, at a birthday party with my young daughters when an elderly babysitter fell over a bench backwards and broke her hip. As soon as she hit the ground, I knew what had happened because once you hear that sound, you never forget it. The second time I heard the "Snap," I also felt it. Falling from a cheerleading pyramid, I shattered my arm, the sound telling me I had broken bones even before the pain set in.

Daddy would never let a minor thing like a leg broken in six places stop him from ice skating again. Physical set-backs are just that: physical. They heal. But he knew that exercise nurtures the spirit. I learned that while I might not skate blissfully through life without injury, I can occasionally glide over the ice on a winter afternoon to bolster my spirits and heal my soul.

20

BAIT BOSS

"It may be doubted whether there are many other animals which have played so important a part in the history of the world, as have these lowly organized creatures."
—Charles Darwin, 1891

Maw-Maw, my paternal grandmother, was as transparent as Saran Wrap. No hidden motives, no mind games, no sharp tongue. She was music and word-play and faith rolled into one smiling, white-haired, wrinkled package.

On the other side of the family tree, the branches weren't so straight. "Nanny," Mother's mother and Daddy's "Frene-my," was a puzzlement. (Can you hear me channeling my inner Yul Brynner? I can still hear him singing "A Puzzle-ment." I can still see Anna in that gorgeous lavender, full-skirted dress on the front of the worn *The King and I* album that we played dozens of times a day. Michele and I could sing every word to every song in that movie without missing a single syllable. That's how I learned the phrase, "'tis a puzzlement.")

Nanny was a puzzlement.

The daughter of an itinerant gambler who grew up in a tough home in a Southern Indiana river town, Iona Bessie Hall was a woman who left home early, married at seventeen, and gave birth to six children, only three who survived. My grandparents told of how my mother, Molly, was the only survivor out of two sets of twins. She had a brother who died shortly after birth, and a previous set of twins had already been born and passed. To his dying day, Baw-Baw, my grandfather, was happy to tell the story of his first daughter's miraculous escape from death.

"Now, your Mother…" he would say in his soft, rolling voice, "weighed only two pounds when she was born, and we didn't think she was going to make it. She went down to just a pound and a half. Now remember. This was in 1931, way before all the fancy medical equipment we have now. Your mother survived only because of a nun named Sister Euphonia."

Baw-Baw's skinny, ruddy face shone bright when he explained. "Sister Euphonia worked at the hospital on the newborn floor, and she took it upon herself to make your mother live. She swaddled your mother real tight in a towel and bundled her into the fold of her big black, billowing habit, keeping her close and warm at every waking hour of the day."

I listened spellbound to Baw-Baw's urgent retelling of my mother's miraculous segue into life.

"Why, at night, Sister Euphonia laid your Mother in a cigar box to sleep because it was the only thing she had small enough!"

Every time I think of this story, the sweet, loamy scent of tobacco envelops me as surely as Sister Euphonia's habit as I see Baw-Baw tapping his pipe and puffing out tobacco smoke. Someday, I hope I will meet Sister Euphonia in the Hereafter and thank her for saving my mother's life.

Baw-Baw talked about Mother's birth, but Nanny was more reticent about the birth of her daughter and the loss of my mother's twin brother.

Nanny could do much more than just birth children. She was a hard worker. Her modest homes were always interesting and beautiful because she had a knack with décor. She sewed beautifully, was a good cook, gardener, and fisherwoman. Her resourcefulness was legendary in our family. During the depression, she picked apples from their backyard, cleaned and polished them, and arranged them in a basket with a pretty cloth underneath before she walked to the train station to sell them. Anything she could do to earn money to help Baw-Baw support the family, she would do.

Her natural beauty and sense of style made her a fantastic saleswoman, and she worked for several decades as a top saleswoman in the jewelry department at Stewart's Dry Goods in Louisville. She was skillful at upselling additional pieces, at knowing what to offer a customer looking for the perfect accessory, and at delivering flattery to increase a sale. When she wasn't working, she was crafting exquisite miniature dolls or painting intricate flowers on china. Nanny had her own kiln and sold her beautiful pieces at shows. She sewed, crafted, and decorated her home with a designer's flair.

Nanny and Baw-Baw's house on Westwood Lane had a focal wall with a gorgeous wallpaper mural. My sisters and I loved to study the picture of an old Southern mansion, complete with white columns, painted onto that wallpaper. The gracious house sat back on a vast green lawn sprinkled with weeping willows set under a pastel blue sky. Nanny's mural was such a bold stroke of artistry compared to the plain and simple, austere "non-decorating" of our house.

When Nanny wasn't working magic with her creative hands, she was camping, fishing, or boating. In their retirement, my grandparents, Nanny and Baw-Baw, spent as much time as possible in their little camper, fishing on the banks of lakes and rivers throughout the Midwest. What a dichotomy. How could she be so glamorous and talented in one moment and then be so outdoorsy and sweaty in the next?

Nanny was a tough lady who overcame a difficult childhood, was strong and independent long before it ever became fashionable, and who attempted things many other women wouldn't. By all accounts, she was a knock-out beauty who kept her hair dyed strawberry-blonde, wore sheer black stockings and skinny high heels well into "old age," and got a speeding ticket for going eighty miles an hour when she was seventy-years-old and the speed limit was fifty-five. She once found a bag of marijuana when she lived in Florida and just had to "experiment" with it so she would know what all the fuss was about. (Did she *really* find a bag of it just lying in the gutter in the early 1970's?)

She attended church weekly, but could snidely deliver barbed comments to unsuspecting victims. Like the time we were with her at a funeral. Someone said, "Hello, Iona. You look great." Her response was a cutting, "Thank you. You've gained weight, too." She belonged to a Sunday School class of older women who sold *knives* as a way of earning money for their charity projects. (She, of course, was the top saleswoman, and they were wonderful, sharp, easy-to-handle knives. But still...)

I knew she loved me, but I couldn't ever forget the time when I was twenty-one years old and at my cousin's wedding. As people were standing in the receiving line waiting to be greeted, Nanny loudly berated me in front of everyone: "Missi. You should be ashamed of yourself. That skirt is just too sheer. Why, people can see right through it. You should know better!"

Mother had bought that pretty, yellow-dotted swiss skirt and top for me as one of my honeymoon outfits. She had also purchased a pale-yellow half-slip bordered in dark beige lace with a matching camisole that I wore with that outfit. No matter what Nanny thought, I was absolutely *not* wearing a see-through skirt without a slip and I was absolutely *not* ashamed of myself. Even my prim and proper Mother had approved the yellow outfit—pretty, stylish, but modest. I can't imagine what set Nanny off that night unless it was the one inch of sheer space between the hem of my skirt and the bottom of my slip.

Humiliated but mad, I got a feeling for how Daddy must have felt when, thirty-years before, Nanny claimed she didn't know his name at the time of his engagement to her daughter. I see how hurt and offended he must have been when after sixteen years of marriage, Nanny accused Daddy of having an affair with a lady in his carpool. Daddy, who was good-looking and friendly, laughing at jokes and spending time driving across the river with two other women, might have been an easy target. We all knew, however, that Daddy was not like that. He was home every evening, like always, smiling, taking us to the pool, working in the yard, or reading the paper in the family room.

Granted, a junior high girl doesn't know much about adult relationships, and I know Mother and Daddy tried to keep it from us, but I know both my parents were furious at Nanny. At church one Sunday, when we attended just like we had every other Sunday for every week of our lives, Mother made sure all of us girls sat on her left. This increased the distance between her and Nanny on the other end of the pew. Daddy was out-of-view behind the altar cloth, singing in the tenor section of the choir. It was the Johnson girls who could feel the ice-cold anger weighing down the air on the pew between Nanny and Mother. During this, I only remember hearing Mother and Daddy talk about Nanny, both of them saying, "Well, we know how she is…"

Since there was nothing to the accusation to begin with, Nanny's implications fizzled like the last spark of a Roman candle fading into a midnight sky.

Barbed tongue aside, my grandmother was also the most talented, energetic, hard-working woman I'd ever seen, and she loved her "grand-kiddos." She and Baw-Baw would take us for Sunday rides after church. Nanny always urged us to be more adventurous than we were, often chiding Mother for being too strict. When Melanie was a prom queen candidate, unbeknownst to my parents, Nanny sneaked my cousin, Julie, into the crowning ceremony to see the results. Melanie wasn't crowned queen, but my cousin still remembers how cool it was to steal into the big, decorated ballroom, hiding with her grandmother like spies behind the potted palms and crepe paper spheres to watch the festivities.

When we were little, Nanny would take each grandchild for a special day with her. She always made sure it was a memorable event. On my appointed day, Nanny took me Woolworth's, where we sat at one of the Formica-covered tables in front of the soda fountain. I had a grilled cheese sandwich and patted my little velvet purse filled with my lifesavings of pennies and nickels while I ate. Nanny patiently helped me count them out so I could "shop." We found Mother a tiny Christmas candle and I bought a roll of butterscotch lifesavers for myself. (Obviously, Nanny made me feel very special. I was only five and can still remember what I ate and what I bought.)

Gorgeous. Talented. Hard-working. Artistic. Fun-Loving.

Outspoken. Judgmental. Difficult. Nanny was a puzzlement, for sure. A kind of living riddle which I often tried to figure out.

A riddle: What do the following words have in common?
Earth. Tape. Ring. Gummy. Book. Grub.

First clue: Children believe that they can play pinochle on your snout.

Second clue: On a beautiful, sunny, spring day, they remind me of my Nanny.

The answer: Worms.

Yes, it's a puzzlement.

What does Nanny's character have to do with those squirmy things that early birds get? Who in her right mind would say that fat, red, slippery worms flopping around in upturned earth, remind her of her grandmother?

I would. (Such a fascinating woman with a million facets to her façade.)

When I was about ten, I remember obeying Nanny's orders to descend the stairs and follow her into the bowels of her basement.

For years my cousins and I had played shuffleboard on a painted court on the tan linoleum of the basement floor during family gatherings, so it's not like I hadn't been down there before. Nanny housed her kiln in a little walled-off room, but there were nooks and cubbies hidden in the recesses of this subterranean warren I had never explored. Weaving around stuff in the basement to a dark corner, I found myself in front of a stack of gray file cabinets.. She stood next to me, regally holding a plastic bowl full of coffee grounds and table scraps like a chalice. "Open the drawer, Miss," she commanded.

I knew better than to hesitate, but I was completely bewildered. What was she hiding in there? Some kind of art project? Maybe a small pet, like a hamster? Shivering with anticipation, I gripped the steely handle.

"Come on, Missi. Let's not take all day doing this!"

A weird but good smell emanated from the second drawer as I pulled it out. A moist, earthy scent, like the garden after a gentle rain. In a million years I wouldn't have guessed that the drawer would be completely packed with brown dirt.

Making a clucking sound with her tongue, Nanny slid open the other gray, metal file drawers. No files. No stationery supplies. No paperwork or pictures or paint supplies. Instead, damp, dense compost overflowed. Each drawer held a moveable, miniature farm.

Nanny's dyed blonde hair was perfectly coiffed. She wore sparkly earrings, rose-colored lipstick, and a pink sweater with beads sewn all over the shoulders. Just like she always taught us to do, she pulled her sleeves way up over her elbows. Then chuckling, Nanny reached in and plunged her brightly painted fingers deep into the dirt.

I couldn't help but cringe. Getting dirt under my fingernails has always grossed me out. But Nanny was grinning as she pulled her dirty hands out of the drawer. Her fingers emerged writhing with hundreds of wiggly, squiggly, squirmy red worms.

I squeaked out a burp of amazement and disgust.

"Look at those, Miss! Aren't they beauties?"

"Ugh. Nanny! What are you doing? They're not 'beauties.'" I recoiled, going queasy at the sight of those things crawling through her fingers. The term "bathing beauties" suddenly mutated in my mind to "baiting beauties."

The worms crawl in. The worms crawl out... The worms play pinochle on your snout...They eat your eyes. They eat your nose. They eat the jelly between your toes.

Gross! Gross! Gross! Lyrics slithered unbidden through the coils of my brain, an "ear-worm" at its fattest, finest best.

"Ah, Miss, but they *are* beauties! They are *great!* You just don't understand what they do. All I have to do is feed them and keep them in the dark. Did you know that they love coffee grounds?"

Seemed to me that anything kept in the bowels of the basement, fed in the dark confines of a locked drawer, and hyped up on rotted coffee-droppings couldn't be all that great.

According to Nanny, she was making a killing at the local bait shops where she delivered her home-grown worms a couple of times a week. Who would have thought that a beautiful, sophisticated woman would be making extra cash dealing worms to dinky little bait shops along the Ohio River? Seemed just a little "underworld" to me, and I kept imagining Nanny as a glamourous spy making the pre-dawn rounds in the river mist, frequenting old gas stations and fishing huts as some kind of "Bait Boss." Her rise in the world of fisherman's food was just another example of my grand-mother's amazing resourcefulness and ability make money out of nothing.

Chutzpah, she had.

I have no idea how long Nanny kept up her worm-works. I don't know what became of the filing cabinets in the base-ment or how much money she made on those nasty night-crawlers. I only know that long after she has departed from this earth, she still haunts me, arising like a smell from the damp earth at the oddest moments. I see her talent fighting with her tongue. Her drive overcoming her demons. Her judgment still hovers near me, but it beats against the force of her love, like a moth beating itself to death against a light.

Nanny's memory lingers on, wiggling forever in and out of my consciousness like those doggone silly worms.

21

INVITATION TO A HERO

"Also, my roses are beautiful. If you were here, I'd give you a bouquet."
—Letter to Missi, May 19, 1992

F ive years younger than my sister, Melanie, and still in that gawky pre-pubescent stage, I was in awe of her friends. Now, as an adult, I realize that the magic of youth and the love of my older sister colored her friends with the glow of heroism. Melanie was the accompanist for her concert choir and madrigal groups, and many of her handsome friends came to our house for school-sanctioned extra rehearsals. I watched those boisterous, testosterone-filled teenage guys with eleven-year-old adoration. As I segued into the teenage years, the luster dimmed and many of Melanie's circle faded from memory as my own friends took precedence, but each spring, even now, I think of Tommy Nolan, a hero whose image will never tarnish.

Every day, as one of her allowance-earning chores,

Melanie was charged with cooking dinner so that it would be ready when my parents returned from work. She performed her duty adequately. Cooking, for her, was a chore; a task to get through. She did it with little thought. One warm spring afternoon in April, Melanie may have regretted her blasé attitude toward meal preparation. That was the day Tommy first dropped by our house after baseball practice.

Never a very attentive cook and flustered by this good-looking ballplayer's unannounced visit to her house, Melanie forgot her job. Instead, she batted her eyes and chatted with the green-eyed Tommy on the front porch. Meanwhile, unattended on the stove, the potatoes burned to a blackened film in the saucepan, and the steak incinerated into a lump of charcoal under the broiler. The stench of burning food wafted onto the porch. Panicked, Melanie rushed squealing into a kitchen filled with tendrils of black smoke. That was the moment Mother and Daddy drove into the driveway after a long day of work.

Daddy, always open and friendly and oblivious to the culinary catastrophe that lay in wait, picked that very day to spontaneously invite the first boy *ever* into our home for dinner. "Tommy, why don't you stay to eat? I'm sure there's plenty."

"Da-Da-Da-Daddy, I may have…um…forgotten to….um…set the timer. I think I got it a little done," Melanie stuttered, classically understating the problem.

"A little done won't hurt anybody! We'll just cut off the dark parts and eat the rest," Daddy insisted with his usual laugh and carefree attitude.

The surprise invitation threatened death-by-embarrassment to my sister. She looked down, clenching her fists at her sides. Melanie had a dark complexion and never blushed, but I could have sworn her eyeballs were turning red. What in the world can you serve to someone when everything has been incinerated? The cheap cut of meat was a hunk of carbon and the thin layer of potatoes scraped off the bottom of the pan tasted like they'd been mixed with volcanic ash. What would Tommy think of this pretty girl with the culinary skills of an arsonist?

That evening my parents, militarily strict when it came to dating and boys, crammed a chair next to Melanie's spot at the kitchen table and made a place in their hearts for Tommy Nolan. Who, after all, wouldn't love a guy who munched hardened black steak and said with a grin, "I like my meat a little crunchy"?

Of course, Melanie couldn't possibly refuse this boy when he asked her to the prom.

Melanie became the princess of my world when she donned her first formal dress, a white chiffon, high-waisted gown tied with a velvet sash and bordered with deep pink flowers. With a little sister's devotion, I thought she was the most beautiful girl in the whole world.

If Melanie was my princess, Tommy Nolan was my idolized-from-afar prince. The high school guidance counselor let Tommy borrow his gold Cadillac to take my sister to the Clarksville High School prom. He drove up in this freshly waxed, shining carriage and emerged with his arms loaded, hardly able to see from behind a tall stack of white boxes as he gallantly charged up the hill on Driftwood Drive.

No wonder he was one of the only beaus to ever win my cautious, distant Mother's heart. I shivered with excitement as he presented one of those big boxes to Mother. She was dumb-founded and stammered a gracious, "Well, I never... The very idea... You didn't have to do this. I can't imagine... Thank you so much," when she pulled the lid off the box to find a dozen, long-stem, pink roses. The same shade of rose-pink climbed up Mother's pale, freckled neck (Who knew that floral bribery was all it took to win her approval?)

If I was excited when Tommy gave Mother a gift, I was absolutely besotted when Tommy handed Melanie a long box. My stomach turned over itself, making me feel like I had inside giggles. Melanie opened her box to a dozen, deep-red roses. I couldn't hear her response for the beating of my own heart. The look between her and Tommy made the mirror hanging behind the piano waver. As Mother stepped into the kitchen to find a vase, Tommy presented yet another box to my sister. It was deep and square, like a treasure box, I thought, as Melanie exhaled a whispery "Ah!" and removed a bouquet of pink and white carnations, topped with a white silk butterfly, and perfectly coordinated with her gown.

Melanie's hand trembled a little as she pinned Tommy's boutonniere on his lapel, but it didn't tremble when Tommy held it throughout the picture-taking that followed. I watched his thumb tenderly caress the top of her smaller, softer hand.

Tommy and Melanie departed for the ball, eyes sparkling like the flashbulbs popping around them, leaving a dewy-eyed mother, two charmed little sisters, and a house perfumed with the scent of roses and the stuff dreams are made of.

Every spring, I think of my sister's boyfriend and how much money he had to earn to pay for those roses, how much thought and effort he put into making a good impression on my mom, how well-mannered, good-natured, and gentle-hearted he was. A week after prom, Tommy dropped by our house on my birthday. (Silly, naïve me, thinking he came specifically to bring me a card, not realizing that he actually came to see Melanie.) It was my twelfth birthday. For the first time, I wore pantyhose instead of knee socks and felt very sophisticated indeed. Tommy, who must have been clued-in by Melanie and was always a model of chivalry, smiled at me saying, "Well, don't you look grown-up!" ignoring the fact that the nylons bagged like elephant skin around my skinny, scrawny legs.

It was Tommy Nolan who ushered me into the realm of romantic, albeit unrealistic expectations and left me with the permanent hope that somewhere out there are sensitive, hard-working teenaged boys who value the affection of mothers, cradle the hearts of girls, and retain the image of hero.

But it was Daddy, with his open heart and father's intuition, who invited a hero to dinner.

22

NO MATTER HOW OLD...

"Life is pleasant. Death is peaceful. It's the transition that's troublesome."
—Isaac Asimov

A strange cough-like sound woke me up the morning after Maw-Maw's funeral. Curious, I walked through the quiet house where everyone was asleep, drawn by the noise I had heard. Maybe it was just one more instance where I was simpatico with Daddy, a bond that drew me to him when no one else heard. Maybe it was just a fluke that I had heard him. (Don't all daughters like to think they're Daddy's favorite?)

It was cold winter night in January, and true-to-his-nature, Daddy had a fire going. The glow of warm embers enveloped the small den.

I stood in the door frame and watched in silence. Daddy was sitting on the hearth, his body heaving with sobs.

My heart lunged. My strong, sweet, singing, laughing

Daddy was crying. Loudly and unapologetically. I had never seen Daddy sniffle, much less weep like this with ragged, raw jags that came from the depths of his body. Knees pulled up, he sat with his head bowed over crossed arms. Should I say something? Should I turn around and leave him to his lonely grief? Should I let him know that I had seen him in this moment of intense private grief?

Stunned by the depth of his sorrow, my eyes teared up. What daughter can stand to see her father cry?

Daddy looked up without surprise, recovering himself. "You know, Miss," he whispered when he looked up at me, his tear tracks reflecting in the firelight. "It doesn't matter that she was ready to go, that I believe she's with God, or that no one can live forever. She was still the only Mother I'll ever have. I said I wouldn't grieve at her death. She was ninety years old and couldn't even remember who I was anymore. For years, she said she was ready to meet her Maker, that all-powerful, mighty God she talked about. But I was wrong about not grieving. It hurts and I'm so sad."

Daddy's honest expression of his feelings humbled me.

Another sob before he uttered brokenly, "No matter how old or senile, no matter how decrepit or how long they've suffered, it is still a loss for those who love them."

What Daddy bestowed that solemn night was a lesson in life and in death, a revelation. Twenty-five years old and newly pregnant with my first child, I had assumed that by the age of ninety, it was time to go. That family would be prepared for them to pass. You can't live forever, right? Daddy's raw emotion was evidence that if you love someone, there will always be grief when they die. No matter how much people say they are ready to go, or how much the people who love them think they are prepared for the loss, the pain is real.

Daddy and Mam-Maw IU Graduation

23

THE PRESIDENT'S OVERCOAT

"Molly and I think this Easter was one of the best we ever had. 'It just don't get any better than that.' How proud we were, too, to have you all at church with us. When I looked out from the choir, I thought what a good-looking group you were, and you are all ours. As my Dad would say, and I quote again, 'The President's overcoat wouldn't make me a vest.' Thank you."
—Letter to Family Groups, April 24, 1995

"Well, for a fat girl, she sure doesn't sweat much," was Daddy's overused joke when he couldn't find anything good to say about a person. Sometimes he said it just to be funny, and he thought this line was hilarious every single one of the hundreds of times he said it. (This was long before "fat shaming" and in repeating the old joke, Daddy never intended to insult anybody. He never even considered that it might be offensive to overweight people.)

"It's not over 'til the fat lady sings," was another adage, stated loud and often.

But the most interesting, and the most puzzling was Daddy's expression: "The President's overcoat wouldn't make me a vest."

"What?"

I didn't understand it until I was an adult, and even then, I had to think long and hard about the meaning of this strange phrase. Daddy said he heard it from his Dad, and he had been born in 1890, so maybe it was a common colloquialism at the turn of the century.

"The President's overcoat wouldn't make me a vest," I repeated, pondering the meaning.

The leader of the free world is an important man—powerful, smart, and very, very proud. His overcoat is huge, protecting his body, and figuratively, the nation. Take that extra-large garment made from yards and yards of fabric, and you'll find that there's not enough material to even make a short, sleeveless vest for a guy whose chest is as puffed up with pride as Daddy's.

No doubt about it. Daddy was always proud of his family.

While pride figured into his chest size, it didn't keep Daddy from wanting us to know our place in the grand scheme of things. Humility and strength were lessons from two ends of the spectrum. Throughout our lifetimes, Daddy would tell us: "There's always someone better-off above you, but there's always someone far worse-off below you." (Richer, smarter, healthier vs poorer, dumber, sicker.) Daddy reminded us that while we may not be the absolute "Best" at anything, we also weren't the absolute "Worst", either. In his mind, there was a kind a magic in being ordinary. Average, common people, not upper-crust, but not trampled on. Neither arrogant nor despairing. Just people accepting who they were and what they had. Dealing with it and moving on.

"Just put one foot in front of the other and take one step at a time," was another life lesson Daddy put into a simple statement. In times of stress, trauma, tragedy, or loss, Daddy pushed us to go forward. Sadness, failure, or loss couldn't smother you if you were forging ahead, leaving your problems behind.

Daddy was a wise man in a simple way. Usually.

From the time we were born, Mother and Daddy raised us to be independent. The Johnson girls knew the unspoken rules: Grow up. Go to college. Leave home. Once you leave home, don't come back. Go out and make your way in the world.

Mel and Molly Johnson practiced the "we-gave-you-wings-now-go-fly philosophy."

In 1979, I had just announced my engagement and upcoming marriage to my church family, the congregation at Centenary United Methodist Church. One Sunday after the service, two elderly sisters, lifelong members, stopped Daddy to comment on my engagement. Neither had ever married or ever left town, and now they were in their late seventies, living in the home their parents had owned for the last century.

"Oh, aren't you and Molly sad about Missi leaving home? Aren't you so sorry to have her get married and go away?" they asked Daddy, leaning in to hear his response, doleful eyes blinking.

Usually charming and sensitive, Daddy smiled and loudly proclaimed what he felt. "Well, the only thing that would be worse is if she never got married and never left home!"

Exactly the wrong thing to say to this particular audience.

The sisters coughed, flushed, and shuffled away. How could they possibly respond?

Most of the time, but not always, Daddy's sayings were words of wisdom.

24

YARD TOURS

"I am sitting on the deck of the USS Mellyford. It is like having another room in your house. It is a beautiful first full day of summer, and I have a red lily with seven blooms right off the deck, like a red candelabra."
—Letter to Missi, June 22, 1993

Remember when you were fourteen years old and you thought that being forced to do yardwork was cruel and unusual punishment? When having to weed the garden was absolute torture? When picking up sticks seemed a gross misuse of your time and talents?

When is it, exactly, that yardwork stops being a job and becomes a pleasure?

Daddy walks around the yard every morning in the summer. What, I wonder, does he find to look at on a daily basis? What does he see that is worthy of such keen observation? Why on earth does he just walk around the yard, his hands in his pockets, his lips pursed in a gentle whistle?

While the lot on Driftwood Drive is a nice-sized, corner-hill piece of land, it is not a big estate. The whole plot, including the house, is less than a quarter of an acre. Yet every day Daddy inspects the property like an estate baron: his landholdings, every inch of his grounds, each blossom, shrub, and blade of grass. He wants us to share in his botanical bounty.

A gambler could make money by betting on how long it takes Daddy to say, "Come see my yard" to any of his three daughters or their spouses. Five minutes or less is the average. If the weather is warm enough, it's a sure bet that Daddy will crook his elbow, link arms with us, open the door, and lead us out, an enthusiastic escort to the gardens on "Bum's Corner."

It is from these "Yard Tours" that I have memorized the details of my childhood home. I can see the huge holly tree in the left corner of the back yard. I know that the fireplace side of the house will always have a two-row planting of tomatoes, peppers, and lettuce. The big blue spruce tree on the hillside of the lot has grown from a measly three-foot shrub that Melanie used to jump over like a champion track star. The first time she attempted to clear that three-foot tall evergreen I was scared to death. Three-foot tall wasn't much shorter than I was, and there was no way I would let Melanie attempt a jump over me. Besides, we all knew how much Daddy *loved* that blue spruce.

"What if she misses and breaks the top off?" I would think, far more worried about the fitness of the fir tree than the safety of my sister.

"I know I can jump over that!" Melanie assured Michele and I, her personal crowd of two cheering fans. We would watch, breathless, as she backed up all the way to the hedge row. She would crouch, push off with her back leg, and run as fast as she could, legs pumping, then leap like a reindeer, sailing over the blue spruce with grace.

That tree is huge and majestic now, standing more than fifty feet tall. (I *know* she can't jump it now!)

The flowerbed around the locust tree in the back yard flaunts red salvia and purple hyacinth. Daddy said that hummingbirds like red salvia, and he was right. The beat of rapid-fire wings and flashes of iridescent green often flicker around that tree. The narrow little bed in front of the porch displays big, crimson geraniums, and next year—based on Daddy's alternating year plans—it will sport big red begonias.

Would I remember that much about our yard if I hadn't been obligated to go with my dad on those occasions when he held out his arm and beckoned, "Come see"?

The exact same words came out of my own mouth just the other day. People say we become our Mothers. I was becoming my Dad, his words channeling through my soul and coming out of my mouth. I had been working all week doing the early summer planting, and I asked my youngest daughter, Cassie, who just happened to be in the kitchen when I stepped in to wash my hands and was the first possible victim of my enthusiasm, to "Come see. Look at the yard." She humored me, nodded politely as I showed her the roses and told her the names and characteristics of each. Smiling a little, she said my idea of putting a birdhouse on a platform was a good one. Bless her heart, she listened to my hopes for more flowers and said it looked nice after I explained all the chores I'd been doing to make it pretty.

Is it a sign of age, (Or maybe wisdom? Maturity?) that I've crossed into Daddy's way of thinking? Every morning, and usually several times a day after that, I walk around the yard checking on the health of each plant. I pluck weeds from the soil. I water the flowers. I contemplate the weather. I plan what to do to the flower bed to make it more beautiful next year. Mulch, rock, and gravel are all subject to my wild imagination and runaway garden plans. I look at nothing and everything, humming while I amble around.

Suddenly, Daddy's habit makes sense. Working the land and surveying the fruits of my labor satisfies me.

When I wield my yard tools, I'm empowered to beautify the world. There's heft and might in hoes and rakes. A kind of "high" exists from choosing the right kind of flower fertilizer and weed killer. Does it make sense that I don't even hate cutting the grass anymore? That I debate the relative benefits of vertical versus horizontal stripes in the grass and then try out new patterns aiming for the most beautiful, but most efficient, way of mowing? My lines aren't always perfectly straight, but the end result is still pleasing to the eye.

Perhaps as we get older, we get more like our parents. Maybe there's a certain time in our life when it's fun to work hard out-of-doors. Possibly, it's just that a sense of place takes on increased importance in our quest to make ourselves a home in this world.

Whatever it is, yardwork is no longer a drag. As Daddy knows, a daily inspection of the grounds is not an eccentric habit of an aging parent. but the right and proper behavior of any respectable adult.

25

MYSTERIES IN AN ELECTRIC
FUNERAL PARLOR

"Thanks, Missi, for listening. Your Mother doesn't know I went to the funeral, and I haven't told her because she just isn't comfortable with it."
—Letter to Missi, October 24, 1990

"Funeral." "My brother." "Mistaken." Only a few of Daddy's words were clear in the garble of voices that floated up the stairs. Everything in between the decipherable words was static.

I was lying in bed in the guest room of my Aunt Carol and Uncle Jim's house. Uncle Jim Goetcheus was manager of various J.C. Penney stores on the east coast in the sixties, seventies, and eighties. The locations they inhabited during those years were fabulous vacation spots for our family. Whenever Mother and Daddy could swing a vacation, Aunt Carol and Uncle Jim loved to wine, dine, and entertain us. Aunt Carol wowed us from the time we got there until the time we left, starting with a "welcome" meal fit for a king on a table set for royalty. She would put small, brightly colored cut-glass goblets at the kids' places because she wanted us to feel like adults, not like children who couldn't be trusted with breakables. Michele and I would crook our pinkies as we drank our 7 Up out of those glorious goblets, grateful we weren't relegated to plastic cups and plates. Then Aunt Carol would carry a large silver tray to the dinner table. On it, a huge head of cooked cauliflower spewed hot cheese sauce from the cored-out middle, the molten cheese sauce flowing down the side. It was both a vegan volcano and a memorable moment. Aunt Carol won my heart forever with her flair for the dramatic.

The Goetcheuses lived in Philadelphia, Washington, D.C., New York City, and the White Mountains of New Hampshire. They moved more times than the marbles on a Chinese Checkerboard. Everywhere they lived became a vacation spot for the Johnson family. Wonderful memories of this fun-loving, upbeat couple fill the travelogue of my childhood. Aunt Carol, Mother's sister, was a fair-skinned, freckle-faced, redhead with a dry, Frasier-like sense of humor and a rumbling chuckle. I was going to be an English teacher, and since that was what Aunt Carol was, I felt like we were simpatico, some kind of language-love automatically binding us together. Uncle Jim was a big guy with eyes that got so large the whites showed all the way around the irises. His emotion didn't show in his even-keel voice. It showed in those vivacious eyes.

When we visited Aunt Carol and Uncle Jim in the Washington area, they took us to see Arlington National Cemetery. My eyes never left the view from the car window as we drove in. The rows of white tombstones assaulted my vision. So many graves, like the earth had suddenly sprouted row upon row of baby teeth. It was more than I could absorb or understand. At the Tomb of the Unknown Soldier, standing in the hot white light of the sun, the power of the ritual hit me. Somber-faced soldiers in full military regalia marched in front of the tomb, presented weapons and clicked their heels. JFK's Eternal Flame amazed me with the idea of "eternal" anything, but also with the amount of "blue" at the base of the flickering fire that day. Hundreds of people gathered around, not one of them making a sound. I don't know how much I understood about the political, military, and historical implications of Arlington, but the reverence, the quiet, the weight of the place was unmistakable.

I was a junior in high school when we visited Aunt Carol and Uncle Jim when they lived somewhere in New York. I only remember how old I was then because I remember wearing my new black and white, zip-out-flat-large-sailor-collar Varsity Cheerleader jacket. Someone walking on the street jibed as they walked by, "Ooooh. Varsity Cheerleader. You think you're hot stuff, don't you?" I kept walking, but yes, I did think I was hot stuff.

That trip, Aunt Carol and Uncle Jim took us to see Radio City Music Hall's legendary Rockettes show. It was a glittery extravaganza with a lot of high kicks and music. Mother kept saying, "Jim, you shouldn't have" after he bought tickets for all of us. I'm sure it wasn't cheap, and it was, indeed, a real luxury for us.

What I remember most on that whole trip was Uncle Jim taking us to the top of the Empire State Building. He put quarters into the rotating telescope so we could look at the city. Michele must have used all the quarters up because when my turn came, the telescope clicked off. Mother was standing nearby, apologetically saying, "It's time to go," and "Oh, Jim, don't worry about it." My good-hearted uncle, though, wanted to make sure I got to see the city, and inserted another quarter into the slot.

"Now, Molly, another couple of minutes won't hurt," he

insisted, the whites of his eyes showing as they opened large, focusing on Mother. "It's just a quarter, Molly!"

Uncle Jim was the only person I ever met who could chuckle, smile, and get his point across without giving offense. He was the kind of guy who would smile and wink at you while slipping a dollar into your pocket, genial and generous.

Aunt Carol and Mother were as different as a chocolate bonbon and a dry piece of rye bread. They may have been sisters, but they weren't anything alike. Aunt Carol cracked jokes and told rollicking stories that ended with that rumbling chuckle of hers. In all my life, I never heard Mother tell a joke or try to make a "funny." Aunt Carol was always making witty remarks. Once, when I was eight and Aunt Carol had just had a baby, my cousin Robbin, we walked into the baby's room and I sputtered, "UGH! It smells bad in here." Aunt Carol quickly shot back, "Well, you know, Missi. The smeller's the feller." I was aghast! Mother and Daddy wouldn't even let us use the word "crap," yet here was Aunt Carol, openly talking about bodily functions and then laughing unashamedly about it. Her ability to do that made her approachable, warm. She was a role model. An idol. A favorite aunt.

Kids and adults loved Aunt Carol and Uncle Jim. They were easy to talk to, had a lovely home, and served wine with dinner, something unheard of at 1708 Driftwood Drive. It was no surprise that the four adults were having animated conversation after the kids had gone to bed. Daddy obviously felt comfortable enough in the ebullient atmosphere of Aunt Carol and Uncle Jim's living room to bare his soul. It was also no surprise that he launched into a story. All I could catch from my bed, however, were snippets of Daddy's conversation: "Funeral." "Brother." "Mistaken."

That night at their house, Daddy's secret came floating to

the surface. The words wafting up the steps were my clues to solving this case. What story could Daddy be telling Aunt Carol and Uncle Jim that he hadn't told us? I pulled at all the strings of Daddy-stories to figure out which one might include the words "Funeral." "Brother," and "Mistaken." Nothing matched. Did Daddy have another brother that died and that he never talked about? Was it possible that there was a man who died and was mistakenly identified as one of Daddy's brothers, i.e., "The Johnson Boys"?

I never did figure it out, and the words left me as I drifted off to sleep. It wasn't until several years later that I learned the whole truth. Sitting around the kitchen table when I was in my twenties, Daddy began to tell the story, even though Mother kept sighing, "Meeeeellllll..." like she wanted him to stop.

He didn't.

Daddy's voice resonated as he took on his "storyteller" mode, putting both hands on the table so he would be ready to gesture. "My Dad died in 1964, of heart problems. The biggest shock of my life came when we were at the funeral home for the visitation. People were coming and going, talking to all of us."

"In walks this woman. She comes right up to me and says in a determined voice, 'I'm here to see my brother.'"

"Her *brother*? What was she talking about? My dad didn't have any sisters." Daddy said.

"I didn't recognize her, and since the funeral home had several sections and multiple services going on, I told her, 'Ma'am, I'm sure you must be mistaken. This visitation is for Henry Johnson.'"

"'I know. My brother *is* Henry Johnson. I want to see him.' She was calm and quiet."

"'But ma'am. There are probably several Henry Johnsons. It's a common name,' I told her," Daddy said.

"'I'm here for my big brother, Henry Johnson,'" the lady declared again. She was looking me right in the eye."

"The thing is…" Daddy paused for dramatic effect. "The woman who came to the funeral home that night was black."

Silence. The group around the table sat stunned, trying to figure out the meaning of Daddy's revelation.

"What? You mean Paw-Paw was black?" I asked. Nothing fit together, and I didn't have paper and pencil to draw out a genealogy chart. Sure, I had read of the mixing of bloodlines and the fact that virtually everyone in our country is a blend of cultures and ethnicity, but *our* family?

Nothing we'd ever heard, seen, or experienced gave us a clue that our family history included African-American blood.

'No," Daddy clarified his statement. "Paw-Paw was not black, but his mother, my grandmother, married a black man after my grandfather died."

"So do we have black blood?" I still couldn't work the ancestry angle in my head.

"No, Miss. We don't. But I do have second cousins who are half white and half black. My grandmother had a second family, so they all share her blood, which means that we're a quarter related."

Man. That was a lot of fractions and numbers. My head was spinning. "Okay. So Paw-Paw's dad died, right?"

"Yep. His name was Henry Johnson, too. Family stories say he was robbing a grocery store when he was shot," Daddy said.

Woah. Now I've got a family full of black relatives and the criminal element of robbery on the white side. Our family was growing more interesting with each passing second.

Curiosity drove me forward. Not horror or shame or anger. Pure, unadulterated curiosity. Fascination with the hidden stories of our family – or any family, for that matter.

It's not like Daddy purposely kept all the skeletons hidden. He had told us about "Moonshine Smitty," the boyfriend of his half-sister, Vada. "Moonshine Smitty" served time in the Federal Penitentiary for running a still, and family legend had it that he made Maw-Maw a gorgeous, beaded peacock purse during his time in the slammer. But good old "Moonshine," who made *likker* in the hills and was apparently good with his hands, couldn't hold a candle to this story. Why had Daddy waited years to come clean? Did he think we needed to grow into it? To hit the magic age of twenty-one before we could properly process the information—as if this story got an "M" rating, "For Mature Audiences Only"?

"Your grandfather was killed while committing a crime?" I asked again, persistent as always, doggedly pursuing truth and clarity so my head could get it straight.

Daddy nodded, his palms facing each other, cutting down towards the table. "That's what they say. I don't know much about it. I suppose that's something nobody wanted to talk about either. I don't know any of the circumstances, and I'm not sure if the robbery occurred in Sellersburg, New Albany, or Memphis."

Mother was looking down at her plate, not engaging in eye contact. Her mouth was set in a tight line, almost a grimace. She probably would have been kicking Daddy under the table to get him to stop talking, but her legs weren't long enough to reach him from her end of the table. I could tell she wanted to.

Even if she had been kicking him, trying to stop Daddy when he was in the middle of the story was like trying to stop the ocean from making waves. He just kept right on talking.

"My grandfather's wife was named Allie. Allie Yarbrough Johnson. And after Henry Johnson died in the robbery, apparently Allie married a black man named Frank Dawson who lived down in the hollow behind Silver Hills. When she did, she took her two sons, David and Henry, my dad, with her. And then she gave birth to six more children with her second husband, Frank Dawson. Same mother. Different father. Half-white. Half-black."

For the first time in my life, the ideas of prejudice and race popped up like pimples on my psyche.

"Uuuugggghhhmm." Part throat-clearing, part cough, part groan rumbled up from Mother's throat.

Never before had I wondered about my parents' outlook on race. Never before had I thought about personal prejudices. We had no reason to talk about race relations where we lived. Clarksville was a small city with a white population of about ten thousand people in 1965, and Blackiston Heights was a tight-knit, white, middle-class suburb. No frame of reference existed for my knowing blacks or Hispanics or Jews. There was one Asian girl a year behind me who I was friendly with. I remember going to her birthday party in the old part of Blackiston Heights and feeling terrible because I couldn't understand her Mother's heavily accented Chinese. She was trying so hard to be nice and have a conversation, and I couldn't comprehend one word. I was forced to resort to frenetic pointing, nodding my head, and smiling instead.

Lack of knowledge is not the same as negative feelings toward other races. We had no hatred or fear, just a total lack of exposure to anyone other than white, middle-class kids. Mother, however, was showing definite signs of prejudice toward blacks, however quiet and internal it might be.

"Tell me again. Who was the woman who came to the funeral home?" I asked, close to getting a handle on the genealogy.

"Rosie. Rosie Edwards." Daddy made the same chopping motion with both his hands as if to emphasize his answer.

"Rosie was the second child of Allie and Frank Dawson. She grew up with my dad. She was younger than he was, but they still lived together in the same house for years with all the other kids."

The ancestral lines were vaguely clear, like looking at a route on a blurry map or glimpsing a road through a dense patch of fog. I'd still have to draw it out to make sense of the newly sprung branch in our gnarled family tree.

"So you found this out at Paw-Paw's funeral?" I'm dogged, if nothing else.

"Yep. It was the biggest shock of my life," Daddy proclaimed.

When Paw-Paw died, I was not quite six years old. I have no memory of anything funeral-related. The only fuzzy memories I have of the big, loose-jowled man we called Paw-Paw is of him giving me candy, Brach's Neapolitan Squares, pink, brown, and white blocks of sugary coconut, and of walking into their living room one day and seeing him lying down on the couch.

As an adult, I've often wondered what memories were made in the minds of the people who were at the visitation that evening amid the questions and shock of Rosie's revelation. If only I could have been a gladiola in a floral arrangement that night at the funeral home in 1964.

How did Rosie's simple statement, "I want to see my brother," impact the family?

All of Daddy's siblings and their spouses and children were at the funeral home ready to bury their father. Uncle Virg and Aunt Edna. Aunt Evelyn and Uncle Charlie. Mother and Daddy. Uncle Elty and Aunt Doris. All white. All conservative. How did it play out? Did they all convene in a conference room? Did Daddy just spread the word quietly, sibling to sibling? Had any of the others known about their Dad's childhood? Did my sweet Maw-Maw know about her husband's past? Did she know Rosie? Surely, as tight as Maw-Maw was with God, she would have welcomed her husband's darker-skinned half-sister, loved her, and appreciated her?

The visitation that night was like few others ever held at that funeral home. The circumstances sound like the beginning of a novel where family members come together and discover a life-altering secret. Only this was real life, not fiction. An underlying buzz of emotion and a current of comments between family members made the somber funeral parlor electric.

Rumors among the roses. Lies among the lilies. Facts among the funeral-goers.

You've got to hand it to Rosie. This strong-minded black woman cared enough about my grandfather to come to a funeral home in 1964 and announce to an oblivious white family that they were, in fact, related.

That night started a new chapter in Daddy's family history. He met, for the first time, his Aunt Rosie, and after that, his half-cousin, Mary Elizabeth, Aunt Rosie's daughter. Over the years, he strengthened his connection to Mary Elizabeth, a lady who filled us in on the details of her family's history, primarily through an article she helped formulate entitled "Dawson's Hollow: An African-American Community in Floyd County, Indiana." Daddy took me to visit Mary Elizabeth when I came home from college because he wanted me to know her, a privilege of Daddy's trust and belief that I was like him, and "I would understand."

Mary Elizabeth and Daddy were friends for the rest of their lives, lunching once in a while, visiting occasionally, and keeping each other informed on the achievements and trials of their families. Two people from different backgrounds who shared a family member. Mary Elizabeth was a sweet presence at both Daddy and Mother's funerals, a reminder of the cross-connections that pull people together throughout the course of human history.

Mother, while she was polite to everyone she met, regardless of race, age, or creed, practiced an external kind of forbearance. On the surface she didn't want to *seem* prejudiced, but an underlying current of shame and a residual distrust had been imprinted on her from her own parents. Daddy, however, was open and honest about his family's history. If it hadn't been for Mother, he would have told the story of finding the other half of his family more often. He would have told more people. He would have spread the message of acceptance loudly and joyfully because all families have secrets hidden in their closets. Daddy, God love him, valued the soul of a person, not the color of her skin.

Rosie Edwards died on October 20, 1990 with services being on Tuesday, October 23, 1990. One day after that, in the wee hours of the morning, Daddy wrote me a letter that I cherish.

4:00 a.m.

Dear Missi,

I couldn't sleep so thought I'd write you a letter since I think you probably would understand.

I went to Rosie's funeral yesterday and am enclosing a copy of the memorial service. It's no big deal, but I suppose it is on my mind, and that is why I can't sleep.

It was a beautiful service in a neat, small, attractive Baptist Church on Rear Market Street in New Albany. There were probably about 50 people there, mostly blacks, with a few whites. The choir and director did a good job, but I felt the piano player was going to break out any minute in a full jazz swing; I'll bet if he wasn't in a church, he could really swing it. There were very few flowers, but at 93 years old, that is understandable.

The immediate family consisted of about eight people, of whom the only one I knew was Mary Elizabeth. When I went in, the lady usher asked me how well I knew Rose. I told her not very well, but that she was my aunt. (The devil made me do it!) She gave me a strange look and asked me if I wanted to sit with the family. I said, "no," that they really didn't know me. I had asked Mary Elizabeth at the funeral home the night before if she would mind if I came to the funeral, and she said, "Oh, I wish you would."

As I sat back in the audience looking at the family with whom we share a common grandmother, I thought about fickle fate and how little control we have over it. I certainly didn't know the circumstances, but there had to be a lot of grief and tears shed in the past in the families.

I thought, too, about how consciously or unconsciously prejudiced we can be. I thought about Bonnie and Bill taking Billy Joe out of the Centenary Kindergarten because there was a black boy in it.

What I really saw was a family saying good-bye to someone they loved. The color of your skin had nothing to do with it. The grief was real.

Thanks, Missi, for listening. Your Mother doesn't know I went to the funeral, and I haven't told her because she just isn't comfortable with it.

It is no big secret, but I guess the less said about it, the better...

Love,

Daddy

MHJ

My memories of Aunt Carol and Uncle Jim and of Mary Elizabeth are always strangely intertwined because it was at the Goetcheus' house that I got my first hint of Daddy's secret. Uncle Jim died of a massive heart attack at the age of fifty-eight in May of 1994. When Aunt Carol died less than six months later of a brain aneurysm, having just turned fifty-eight, the family was struck dumb with loss and grief.

Mother and Daddy are both gone now. Mother no longer grits her teeth or kicks Daddy under the table whenever he happily begins the tale of his black family. (God, after all, already knows, so there's no need to keep it quiet.)

Rosie's daughter, Mary Elizabeth Edwards Garvin Mimms, has passed, taking her sweet smile, her shared ancestry, and her affection for Daddy with her.

Daddy's wolf-bait story and historical anecdotes of diphtheria outbreaks and family suicides are all interesting. All are important.

But of all Daddy's stories, Rosie's is the most important. It's the one tale in the Johnson Family Chronicles that shouldn't be forgotten, ignored, disputed, or hidden.

A true story of one good woman who built bridges with courage. A real-life tale of one good man who overcame prejudice with love.

26

THE YEAR I TRULY BELIEVED

*"They err who think Santa Claus enters through the chimney. He
enters through the heart."*
—Charles Howard, *Legendary Locals of Orleans County*

"Mommy, look! He's HERE! Mommy! Can you believe
it?" Katie, a blonde, wispy-haired five-year-old
bounced up and down on Gramps' hearth.

Cassie, her three-year-old sister, sat next to her, smiling
in that big-grinned, full-toothed, tight smile that only a
toddler can manage.

Their eyes were huge and shining, big as lighted
windows. Their pink cheeks glowed. They wore matching
peach sweatshirts, each hand-painted with a big snowman.
Both girls were laughing, bubbles of joy popping out of their
round-O mouths, watching in amazement as he walked in
the family room door. Transfixed by the sight.

So was I.

It didn't matter that I was a college-educated, thirty-one

year-old working woman who understood reality. An involuntary gasp still escaped my own mouth. He *was* here.

No doubt about it. He had to be real. It had to be him.

Santa Claus had come.

"Ho, Ho, Ho! Katie and Cassie! Have you been good girls this year?" his voice boomed, deep and jolly, across the small family room. It bounced around the corners and flittered through the flames of the Christmas Eve fire. He wore red velvet trimmed in curly white fur.

The deep voice resonated as it asked the two transfixed girls questions: "And how, young ladies, was your trip from Kentucky?" "And I hear you did swim team this year?" "Tell me, Katie and Cassie, has your mom been good this year?"

The dewy-eyed duo giggled and stuttered like a flock of twittering birds, unsure how to answer any questions asked by this happy giant standing in front of the fireplace.

I secretly worried they'd report that I'd been a bad girl this year and that this, the "real" Santa, would leave me a lump of coal. Santa, true to his jolly nature and famous powers of intuition, must have glimpsed my uncertainty. His big red hands pushed a bag full of cookies into my hands before handing a bag to each of the girls, rumbling, "Ho, Ho, Ho! Tookie...I mean Mrs. Claus, made those specially for you!"

He patted each girl's small blonde head, gave a hearty wave, and turned, lumbering and laughing through the narrow doorway into the kitchen, "Ho, ho, hoing" all the way.

When he had disappeared into the frosty air of our front porch, we noticed the crisp, clean imprints of his big black boots on the carpet. I never did figure out where the sound of sleigh bells came from or why the family room suddenly smelled like gingerbread and vanilla. It must have been those cookies made by "Tookie." (How privileged we were to know

Santa's nickname for his wife and the lady responsible for the culinary side of Christmas! "Tookie of the cookies" sounded right.)

Like the girls, I was unable to stop laughing, the eye-watering, belly-shaking, gasping-for-air kind of laughter. I had never before seen Santa so up close and personal, appearing right in our family room the Night Before Christmas. My daughters had never been so utterly enamored with anyone before now. I had never truly believed. Until now.

Dickie Pope had been our next-door-neighbor for the last twenty-five years. He was a huge, burly, red-faced, white-bearded guy who worked the barges that flowed up and down the Ohio. He traveled a lot and wasn't always home, and his three boys, Mark, Steve, and Chris, were each one year younger than each of the three Johnson girls. Like us, the Pope boys were all grown and gone from home. Daddy must have told Dickie that I was coming home with the kids for Christmas. Some kind of secret neighbor-notification must have existed for Mr. Pope to time his visit so perfectly, exactly when my daughters were quietly sitting on the edge of the fireplace.

Dickie's Santa charade was an act of kindness and joy that I will never forget, but it also brought back the guilt of youth. When we were very young, right after both families had first moved onto Driftwood Drive, for some odd and errant reason, I decided I would taunt Stevie Pope. Why, I'll never know. He was a cute, freckle-faced, sandy-haired little boy who never did me any harm—until the day I decided I was going to insult him and his dad.

Michele and I were standing guard at the mouth of our open garage. Chris and Stevie stood in mirror image of us, facing us down. Somehow, we got into a word war. Believe me when I say I was only six and have no memory of what I said. I know it was something mean and that I threw in the classic "call to brawl" with whatever insult I had hurled. I jeered, "And your Dad, too!"

Stevie was a sturdy fellow, and when he pulled his elbow back and propelled it forward in a sucker punch to my gut, I felt it. Never mind that I thoroughly deserved it. I went screaming to Mother who had Daddy talk to Dickie so he would talk to Stevie, and it wasn't even his fault. I still feel bad about the fact that I insulted the nice kid next door and his dad, Dickie Pope, who gave me one of the most wonderful memories of my adult life.

The year that our neighbor came into our lives as Santa Claus is the year I *truly* believed. It was also the year I realized that while I thought my dad hung the moon, other kids had dads who knew how to sprinkle stardust, too.

ELEVEN DAYS

"There's something special about a grandmother's house. You never forget how it smells."
—Frederik Backman

The house itself quivered with Nanny's presence when Melanie and I stepped in the door. It looked like her. It smelled like her. It held memories of her. My sister and I looked at each other, eyes wide. We both felt it. This was Nanny's house, and she would never set foot in it again.

Never again would Nanny host large family gatherings at the house on the Westwood hill, cranking homemade ice cream for all the hungry grandkids. She would no longer plant flowers, fix her frequent Spam-with-Tomato-Catsup-Sauce, (the relic of Depression-Era cooking,) or erect those gorgeous Christmas trees, covered with hundreds of ornaments and colored lights, glowing like a nuclear arsenal. She wouldn't serve her pimento cheese in the purple, hand-painted sleigh dish, or pour wine in those gold-edged glasses.

No more sitting on the porch gazing out at the huge weeping willow.

Memories of Easter egg hunts, hide-and-seek games, and cousins running around the willow tree hit us with force. Nanny was responsible for bringing the family together for birthdays and holidays where Uncle Bill, Aunt Bonnie, and the four Wilson cousins connected with Mother and Daddy and the three of us. Uncle Bill wanted to be playing golf, but Nanny wouldn't take "No" for an answer. It was her way or no way. She had been a mighty matriarch.

Nanny was not the stereotypical, white-haired granny with a docile nature and a propensity for knitting and cookie-baking. She was a force to be reckoned with— energetic, beautiful (even as an older woman), and so very talented. She would have been livid if anyone guessed her true age, a well-guarded secret kept hidden by many "white lies" beginning when she was sixteen. Nanny didn't enjoy her own birthdays and scornfully rejected the knowledge that she was getting older. She dressed with style, accessorized with aplomb, and rocked a pair of heels every Sunday, showing off slender legs that took the focus off of her widening middle. No frumpy clothes or sensible shoes for her. Age was one gift she did not appreciate.

Melanie and I stood in the silent kitchen, thinking in tandem: "Too bad she didn't appreciate growing older. Now she won't have a chance to do it."

Just a few weeks before, the extended Johnson clan had all purchased tickets to see the Broadway musical *Cats* at Butler University in Indianapolis in celebration of Nanny's birthday. Even though she hated getting older, she was happy to join the Broadway-show-bound crowd. She did enjoy a party!

One day my beautiful Nanny was vital and strong. The next, she fainted while at the beauty parlor getting her hair styled and her nails manicured for this Johnson family outing.

Clammy, sick, and vomiting in the bathroom of the salon, Nanny had fainted, but not before she asked them to call Daddy. From that day forward, the rest of her life was spent in the hospital. A brain tumor that doubled in size every other day was eating away at her complicated mind. Of course, all kinds of friends and relatives, including her "grand-kiddos," stunned by her sudden and inescapable decline, would sit with her after she'd been moved to a nursing home, talking and visiting while it was still possible.

Time was short. One day, Melanie came from her home in Indianapolis while I came up from Madisonville, Kentucky to be with Nanny. We sat together at Nanny's bedside, talking with the Grand Dame of our family. Nanny wore a nightgown ensemble in her favorite color of rosy pink, with a robe that had long, draping sleeves edged with lace. Because of the tumor, one side of her body didn't work well, and when her droopy arm let the lace of her sleeve dangle in her coffee cup, Nanny became aggravated. She immediately asked us to get a washcloth dipped in cold water so we could clean her up. No matter what your health, appearances were important.

Shaking the finger of the hand that still worked, Nanny pointed at us and hissed, "Whenever you can, you help those old people." She nodded toward the hallway and the occasional passing wheelchair as if "those old people" in the same nursing home as she was in, were totally different from her. In her mind's eye, she was still fit and able to do as she pleased. She would never acknowledge that she was one of those old people, dying and infirm.

"I want you both to go to my house and get one of the china dolls I've made over the years. Hear me? Just go on in and choose the one you like best." Brain tumor or not, Nanny could still command action.

So we did as we were told, traveling the short distance to Nanny's house.

There we stood in her darkened kitchen, hit by a sense of loss as noticeable as Nanny's presence had been. Whispering rooms reminded us that this was a house made into a home by thousands of small touches: her still-life watercolors, her doll collections, her china-paintings, her wall mirrors ornately framed with the Florida seashells she loved to gather and had so lovingly glued in the perfect arrangement of color, shape, and size. Her new sunporch glistened with inexpensive furniture made sophisticated by natural plants, sunlight, and the use of her artist's eye. Her craft room was filled with snippets of material, rolls of lace, screwdrivers, hammers, and glue guns that emanated her belief: "With a little resourcefulness and hard work, you can make anything beautiful."

Nanny's love of exquisite things stemmed from her poor childhood, but it also came from an innate talent for seeing color and form. Her life was spent imparting beauty to her family. Not a day goes by that I don't notice something that Nanny made for me. One year, she made each granddaughter a gorgeous, decoupaged purse. To call it a "purse" is so below the artform she achieved. Mine is an octagon shaped wooden hull, with town buildings running all along the bottom edge. Beautiful gold clasp, each panel meticulously fitted with a green-velvet lining and finished with a tag that says, "Handmade with love from Iona." Each daughter and granddaughter got a different design, ten purses in all. And here's the kicker. Each purse took fourteen coats of varnish. It's a feat that I didn't really appreciate at the time, but looking back at it now, I am struck dumb by this thing of beauty and the time she spent crafting it.

An exquisite candy dish, a teapot hand-painted with forget-me-nots, and a sugar and creamer set detailed with intricate pink roses grace my china cabinet. Miniature vignettes of dolls in plexiglass boxes, extravagantly costumed, adorn my piano. My grandmother gave us all something of herself in the things she made for us. When Michele got married, Nanny crafted a gorgeous miniature doll scene, replicating Michele's wedding dress so exactly that the ribbons on the veil of the doll were proportionate to the ribbons on the veil Michele wore.

When Nanny went to Hawaii, she was attracted to the applique-style quilting of the islands. Nanny, who knew there was nothing she couldn't do, crafted nine beautifully wrought Hawaiian blocks in bright, solid-color fabric when she got home. After Nanny died, Mother found those blocks when she was cleaning out Nanny's house. In Mother's thoughtful, always-focused-on-heritage way, she had them put together, bordered, hand-quilted, and bound. That quilt is a fabulous example of the Hawaiian artform. It is also my legacy gift from Nanny, to Mother, to me. The flamboyant, flagrant yellows and greens and oranges of the quilt remind me of Nanny. Bold. Beautiful. Boisterous.

Nanny's never-ending patience and resourcefulness in creating things of beauty were an example to us. To this day, when I don't have enough money to decorate the way I'd like, I hear myself saying, "Now what would Nanny do?" Somehow, the answer always comes, as if she's sending me creative ideas through telepathy.

As a craftswoman, Nanny created works of art. As a grandmother, she taught the love of beauty, a gift far more valuable than the keepsakes she left behind.

Nanny died eleven days after her diagnosis.

Don't tell her that you know, but she was seventy-seven years old.

"FOOD, GLORIOUS FOOD…."

"I know summer must be almost here, because I just picked enough lettuce for wilted lettuce salad and cut a beautiful Tiffany rose which I placed in the middle of the kitchen table.

Ah, food! Today we're having pork roast, mashed potatoes, creamed corn, wilted lettuce salad, and ice cream with strawberries. Come on over. The oven's set and everything will be almost ready when we get home from church. Dr. Nale wants me to watch my cholesterol and maybe lose a little weight, and for me that's not easy."
—Letter to Missi, May 23, 1999

Daddy's most noticeable sin was gluttony. "Foodie," "connoisseur," and a "gourmand" are all nice titles, but they would be misapplied to him. Those words imply that Daddy would search for the best quality, out-of-the-ordinary, elevated kind of food, savoring fine recipes and searching for great cuisine. Nothing was farther from the truth. Daddy would eat anything, anywhere, any time.

Take, for instance, the time when much of the younger family—some of the grandkids and their children—were gathered to celebrate a great-grandbaby's birthday. Chad and his wife Chrissie hosted, and Mother and Daddy, a.k.a., "Gramps" and "Grammy," had come up from Clarksville to Indianapolis for the party. "Gramps" who was approaching eighty, post-stroke and well into diabetes and heart disease, walked around the house exploring. In his own little world, he liked to look out the windows, check the layout of the house, scope out the landscaping. Ambling through the house was like taking his own private tour. The entire family was so used to Gramps wandering that no one ever worried about it.

Eventually, Gramps sauntered into the room where the next three generations of his family was gathered, happily munching on some new treat. "Yummmm," he said "This stuff is pretty good. Kind of unusual, but nice and crunchy."

Chrissie, the grand-daughter-in-law and owner of the house, looked up at Gramps, her big brown eyes widening in alarm. Her strangled hiccup alerted the others that something was wrong.

"Gramps! Hey, Gramps!" she shouted above the din because Gramps was practically deaf. "Where did you get that?" She gestured to Gramps' hand so he could see what she was asking.

"On the counter in the utility room. I hope you don't mind." He smiled. "Why?"

"Because, Gramps, it's CAT FOOD!" Chrissie roared, both amused and appalled.

Laughter erupted. Embarrassed giggling from the little kids. Streams of undiluted hilarity from the women. Hoots and guffaws from the grandsons, never shy about teasing

Gramps. "Bet there's a tiger in your tank now, huh, Gramps?" Josh joked.

A nonplussed Gramps shrugged. "Well, it tastes pretty good. Really, it's not bad. You ought to try it," he proclaimed loudly, continuing to crunch contentedly while his mortified family looked on.

THROUGHOUT MY CHILDHOOD, DADDY USUALLY COOKED THE meals. His phrase for it was "chief cook and bottle washer." Mother, while she could perform those duties if she had to, saw meal preparation as a chore and was famous for frying tiny, thin hamburgers so crunchy it was like biting into gravel. (No doubt due to her lifelong fear of trichinosis.) Mother only ate because she had to, not because she enjoyed it.

Daddy, however, ate with gusto. He started thinking about the evening meal as soon as he woke up, and sometimes he'd wake up in the middle of the night and plan the next day's menus. No fancy recipes or expensive ingredients needed. They were throw-together, one-pot, simple meals. Good country cooking. Meat. Potatoes. Vegetables. No exotic ingredients. No fancy combinations. No wild spices.

The Johnson family ate that good country cooking around a kitchen table with a seat assignment that must have been carved into stone and drummed into our brains as a commandment. For the more than fifty years that Mother and Daddy occupied the house on Driftwood Drive, we girls never ventured to sit in a different place than the one we occupied as kids.

In 1963 when the house was built, room dividers were all the rage. Other kids' houses had cool spindles that rose from the half- walls to the ceiling, and I was always a little disappointed that our divider wall was plain and simple, without upright balusters. Our austere divider wall separated the eat-in area of the kitchen from the living room. The table was crammed horizontally into a tiny area tacked onto the end of our galley-style kitchen. (It would have fit better if Mother placed it vertically into the alcove, but for some reason, she wouldn't ever change the rotation of the table even though my sisters and I suggested it many times over her lifetime.) Because of this arrangement, you had to hold your breath and flatten your body to the size of a rubber band to get between the corner of the kitchen table and the refrigerator.

Daddy sat at the head of the table, right in front of the den door. Mother sat at the opposite end, and Melanie reigned supreme by herself in front of the kitchen window. Michele and I, always partners in crime, were placed next to each other, across from Melanie. I sat closest to Daddy on his right hand, feeling special, because I had heard and under-stood the Sunday school lesson about the beloved disciples who sat at the right hand of God. (I'm sure the arrangement was just luck, but the mind of a child is a funny thing, and it added to my delusion that I was the favorite daughter.)

In the days of bright white appliances, we got a new oven. Daddy was ecstatic when he discovered that it had a dial with a function called "Time-Bake." With this new-fangled gadget, he could set the time the cooking would start and end. He could turn the knob to a time and the magic oven would come on while we were at church and go off when the service was over. *Voila!* Our noon meal was ready when we came home, always ready to eat whatever Daddy had concocted that morning.

After church Sunday dinners, Mother would command us to load some records onto the old turntable crammed into the corner of the den. Soon the orchestral strains of "The Grand Canyon Suite" or the "1812 Overture" would warble through the kitchen. When Michele was four, rocking her dark curls and feeling the rhythm, she knocked over her pale pink Tupperware cup, spilling her milk across the table as she gestured to the music of the "Grand Canyon Suite", an action that foreshadowed her later notable college adventures. She became a Red Stepper at Indiana University with the ability she gained at the dinner table to rock a tune with her body.

Discussion of all subjects happened at the Sunday dinner table, including the possibility of ghosts, ancestral stories, and current events. Giggling fits sometimes erupted when Michele and I would shake with uncontrolled mirth, often for no real reason at all, and we'd struggle to "settle down!" as Mother scolded or be forced to forgo dessert.

Sunday music and conversation sessions were often served with stewed chicken, one of Daddy's favorites. All he had to do was throw a chicken in the pot, chop potatoes, carrots, and onions, and fill with water. Let the pot simmer slowly on the stove while we were gone to church, and, "Ta Da," he would yodel when we got home, "Dinner's ready!"

Swiss steak was another "go-to" entree. Daddy would take an inexpensive cut of meat, flour it, brown it with onions, and then pour several cans of chopped tomatoes over it. We had a heavy, oven-proof metal pan that would slow bake that steak for several hours until the tomatoes and drippings formed a thick, tangy sauce and the meat was tender enough to cut with a fork, no matter how cheap the cut of beef.

One of the meals he considered best for a cold winter's day was a pot of chili. It wasn't until I was an adult that I found out that for most people, chili was just beans, sauce, and meat. For the Johnsons, chili was in actuality, "Chili-Mac," made with lots and lots of spaghetti mixed in with hamburger. For some unknown reason, my kid's palate detested beans. When we had chili, I would pick each burgundy, kidney-shaped blob out of my spoon so that I was only eating the noodles, the burger, and the sauce, leaving the bottom of my bowl filled with orphaned beans. Our family version of chili figures into Johnson legend since that's the meal that had been prepared the night Daddy broke his leg. Mother had cooked a big pot of Johnson-style chili, orange Jell-O with mandarin oranges, and bought frosted brownies at Williams' Bakery, intending to warm us up after a cold January day of ice skating at Uncle Virg's farm.

Good behavior meant that if we ate all our dinner, drank all our milk, and refrained from undue silliness, we'd get a special treat. Daddy would drop a couple of tablespoons of his coffee into those tall, pastel, Tupperware cups. He'd add a splash of milk, a teaspoon of sugar (no doubt my sugar addiction was learned from Daddy), and Michele and I would think we were sophisticated, grown-ups, crooking our little fingers as we slurped down the cafe au lait. Such a simple thing, really, but such a lasting memory.

Daddy was happiest when he could eat a cookie, a slice of pie, or a hunk of cake. If no desserts were nearby, he would bake one so he could eat it. The kitchen was often a mess of flour sprinkles and berry juice dribbled on the white-and-blue patterned linoleum floor. At Christmas, he would hover around the snack table, eating dozens of treats, always going back for more. For years, I made Haystacks at Christmas because he said he liked them. Haystacks are chow mein noodles thrown into a melted pot of butterscotch chips and then mounded on wax paper until they dry. Really, he liked everything, so I don't know why I believed my Haystacks were special. He was also known to say that he liked brownies, snickerdoodles, sugar, oatmeal raisin, chocolate chip, peanut-butter, white-macadamia-nut cookies, Rice Krispie treats, cupcakes, pastries, pies, cakes, fudge, and virtually every kind of sweet known to man.

If there ever was a love affair, it would be between Daddy and Bob Evans. Not Bob Evans the man, but Bob Evans the restaurant. After he retired from his job and while Mother was still working, Daddy would get in the car and take the short drive down the road to Bob Evans in Clarksville. It's impossible to know how many dozens of eggs or how many gallons of coffee he consumed there, but he never lost the pleasure in having a good breakfast at his favorite restaurant. When we visited, Daddy would be so proud to introduce his family to Faye, the elderly little lady who hostessed there. He presented us to the waitress, to the other "regulars" he knew sitting in nearby booths, and to the cashier at the register when we paid the bill, telling her, "This is my daughter and her husband, and they're taking me out to breakfast today," as if this were a major source of pride.

Eating eggs with abandon, slathering jam on toast, and slurping coffee, Daddy was a messy eater, oblivious to the drips and drabs that ended up on his clothes. Mother gritted her teeth when she saw Daddy after a meal, unable to ignore the grease smear, gravy drip, or construction-yellow egg spot on Daddy's shirt. Yep. Daddy could wear an egg stain with the best of them.

Bob Evans' gift cards were all that Daddy really wanted or cared about receiving as gifts, so for many years all three daughters kept him supplied. Were we enabling his food addiction? Probably. Would he have eaten there anyway? No doubt about it.

When he was young and healthy, Daddy was never still, always exercising, running, playing tennis, swimming, and gardening, so his eating obsession didn't affect him much. By the time he was in his seventies, after his stroke and lacking the agility he once had, Daddy was barrel-shaped. A broad chest descended into a large round middle, not unlike Santa's bowl full of jelly. Somewhere over time, he had developed diabetes, a condition he paid absolutely no attention to, eating whatever he wanted, whenever he wanted, with his usual abandon. It drove us crazy, my mom especially, but we learned to ignore the sound of Mother's irritated nasal droning, "Meeeeellllll...." whenever Daddy scarfed down pie, scooped huge servings of food on his plate, or went back for second or third helpings.

One year at Christmas, Daddy ate so much he got cold and clammy and stumbled to the bathroom to be sick, not an unusual occurrence in his later years. Such episodes frustrated his family. With just a little bit of self-control, just a tiny nod to his diabetes, just one iota of common sense, Daddy could have avoided getting ill.

Too much food and too many cookies took a toll. To be sure, the rise of blood sugar is directly linked to the input of sweets. The sin of gluttony does have consequences.

Daddy's zest for living—that innate urge to take everything in and to enjoy everything—drove him to eat abundantly, deriving a pleasure from food that few of us will ever know.

29

YOUNG AT ART

*"p.s. Pardon the envelope. It's all I could find. There's nothing like
polka-dots for a casual effect. Absolutely nothing."*
—Letter to Molly, May 12, 1952

D addy wasn't God. Even so, the year after I divorced, he
made me a man and then hand-delivered him to my
front door.

I was living in my little house on Conran Avenue where I
kept my own pretty little garden in the back yard and grew
roses on the chimney-side of the house. On one of Daddy's
visits, he got out of his old car and stumbled to his trunk,
calling for me the whole time. "Missi Ann! Come see. Have I
got a man for you!"

Cradled in Daddy's creative arms was a three-foot tall
man made of terra cotta planting pots. A standing robot of
clay, flowerpots were glued together to form his joints. He
had legs, arms, a pot-bellied torso (excuse the pun) and a big
pothead (excuse the pun again). Daddy had strung the pots

on thin pieces of rebar and then painted, glued, and embell-ished those pots to mold him into a little man.

I couldn't help but smile. Daddy's love of gardening had magically morphed into a guardian of the garden. After I had debated between Perry, Porter, and Parker, I simply named him Pat the Pot Head, watcher for weeds, fighter for flowers, and protector of plants.

All of his life, Daddy dabbled with art, his joie-de-vivre dribbling out of his paintbrush or waltzing out of the projects from his workbench. Maybe he could create such fun stuff because he didn't really care what other people thought. He wasn't a trained artist of any sort, and he defi-nitely wasn't following any artistic principles or rules of the craft. He was just doing it to please himself, fueling his own fire in the process. His creative spark burned bigger and brighter than most, and we all benefitted from its glow.

When we were little and had a big snow, we would wait until Daddy got home from work because he would take us out to play. Everybody else's yards flaunted snowmen. But ours? Daddy built "snow-critters." Once a big bunny, at least six feet tall with big ears and a huge snowball for a tail, stood guard in front of the bedroom windows. Once, when we ran outside ready to build a snow creature, Daddy declared we'd have a duck. "A Snow Duck," he laughed.

We didn't care that the entire concept of our "snowbird" was weird to everybody else. To us, it was magic formed with ice and white, flakes and frost, and the touch of our Daddy's hands.

Daddy built with more than snow. He designed and then hand-painted pretty little birdhouses in all shapes and sizes. Occasionally, he would sell some of them, but mostly, he gave them away. To his family. To his friends. To the shut-ins or elderly or ill that he so often visited. Each grandchild still has a birdhouse or a Christmas ornament or a painting by

Mel Ford, Daddy's nom de plume. All of his daughters have something hand-crafted by Daddy, our own genuine piece of folk art. Depending on the piece, we might term it as unique, classic, artsy, or downright eccentric, like the giant wooden, puppet-like flat figure with movable joints Daddy found at a yard sale somewhere. He dragged that odd thing home, painted a woman's dress on it (in bright pink), made her a face, and printed in big black letters, "SALE" across her bodice. Whenever Daddy had a yard sale, he planted that wooden strumpet at the entrance to Blackiston Heights. Believe me, it got people's attention.

My favorite artsy piece made by Daddy was a piece of jewelry. Years ago, after their trip to Italy, Daddy had some foreign coins he couldn't spend in the U.S. He took those coins, drilled holes in them, and made gifts for his girls. Mine was a shiny silver coin with a gold border strung on a long silver chain, a timeless piece of jewelry that still looks good today. Whenever I wear it, I think of my clever father who knew how to take a simple object and turn it into something meaningful, imbuing it with joy, helping it find a beauty of its own.

His creative talents were on display in the basement of Driftwood Drive. Originally, it was nothing but a large, open space with dark gray concrete walls. Then Daddy had an idea. He framed the basement so that it was divided down the middle. One side of the divider was utilitarian: the water-heater; the washer and dryer; storage; a drying rack; Daddy's workbench. Boring stuff.

The public side of the basement was anything but boring. It looked like the backyard of a house. On the divider wall, Daddy glued panel after panel of fake white brick onto the walls. He built windows into that wall, and underneath them, he hung flower boxes with artificial red geraniums. Shake shingles were attached to a roof he put on the walls that extended from below the ceiling for a couple of feet. Along the longest wall, which he painted sky blue, he built a white split-rail fence and placed fake birch trees behind it. The big metal shell-shaped outdoor chairs that Mother bought with her first paycheck in 1952 doubled as décor and seating. The concrete floor was covered in a peel-and-stick tile with an embossed pale blue and white fleur-de-lis pattern, a fancy patio look.

Daddy's backyard basement held more gatherings than I can count. Graduations, birthdays, Christmases, Easters. Tables for wedding gifts. A play area for grandchildren. Daddy designed creative square footage needed for an ever-growing family.

"*I had a watercolor accepted for the 'Young at Art' exhibit. I was surprised that it was such a show. Had my picture taken with the Mayor of Louisville. It was fun.*" Daddy's letter from June 22 of 1993 said. His painting of "Poros, Greece" was done using a photograph that he had taken on their trip to Greece.

Of all of Daddy's many endeavors, my favorite is the pen and ink sketch that hangs in my house now. It is dated November 27, 1955. It's a charming picture of a mother deer and her fawn, standing, face-front, looking at the artist. My sister Melanie would have been three years old, and my parents would have been going through the "miscarriage" phase of their marriage. They had three pregnancies that didn't make it to full term in a five-year period before I was born. Maybe that artwork had been Daddy's way of reassuring Mother that she had one sweet babe. Maybe making that picture helped him to come to terms with the idea that one child might be all they'd ever have. But it is lovely, a piece of art filled with a part of his heart.

Pat the Pot Head succumbed to the ravages of age and a big storm that knocked him silly, breaking his legs and shattering his head. Only one waving arm remained intact as I sadly carted him to the garbage can. Gone, but not forgotten. Just one of many reminders of another far bigger, far better man who enjoyed puttering with pots and paint and plants.

"Young at Art," indeed.

Friends and family enjoyed Daddy's creative, whimsical projects and his artistic talent, but there was something they appreciated much more.

Those who knew him envied his art of living.

30

REAR-GUARD

"She did not stand alone, but what stood behind her, the most
potent moral force in her life, was the love of her father."
—Harper Lee, Go Set a Watchman

Melanie had the epic sixth-grade battle with Gail Wilkins, who pushed and shoved her and wouldn't let her get in the mirror. When she told my parents about it, Daddy told her that she'd have to learn to take up for herself and not get pushed around.

"Next time Gail starts to bully you, Melanie, you just go right ahead and slap her."

Melanie did. My parents got called to school. In the days before "zero-tolerance," Daddy defended Melanie's actions, placing blame on himself. The school accepted the explanation. Gail Wilkins never bothered Melanie again.

Michele had her heroic battle with a first-year high school teacher. A senior, Michele had several years of experience and was scheduled to be the editor of the school yearbook. The new teacher, who didn't know a thing about journalism, was assigned to the project, but she resented Michele for her knowledge and ability to get things going, with or without her. She accused my sister of insubordination and causing trouble in the classroom. Mother and Daddy went to school. Daddy defended her, and Michele was the first student ever allowed to withdraw from a class with an *A*.

I had my own fight. When I divorced my first husband after eighteen years of marriage, my family was horrified. Not only did they love my ex, but they didn't know any of the underlying factors. (Nobody really knows what goes on between two people when they're behind closed doors.) My whole family believed that good, decent women didn't file for divorce. The silence that surrounded me was devastating. For an entire year, the only person who visited me, talked to me, or supported me was Daddy.

He made a special trip up to Danville, in his barely-running old car, to be with me. Checking out the little house I had purchased and moved into with the girls, making sure I wasn't losing my mind, determining my strength and my commitment to my decision, Daddy stood in front of me, put both his hands on my shoulders, and looked me straight in the eye. "Miss, I only want you to be happy. If you think this is the right thing for you to do, I support you."

I didn't blink. It was right for me in a way that felt wrong to everyone else, even Daddy. But he, alone, understood that I had to follow my own course and supported me all the same.

Daddy always had our backs.

31

BLUSTERY WINTER BLUES

"No one ever told me that grief felt so much like fear."
—C.S. Lewis

"Missi. Daddy's in the hospital. We think he's had a stroke."

Melanie's phone call came on a cold January day in 1997, reaching me just after I had stepped out of the classroom where I had been teaching. The news shattered me. For the first time in my life, I experienced the sudden and almost tangible fear that life would never be the same. For the first time ever, my normally buoyant and cheerful nature struggled to lift me. That winter, I did not want to get out of bed.

It's not like I hadn't worried about Daddy's health as the years progressed. His eating habits, his love of fried foods, his penchant for cake before bedtime, his reliance on heavy doses of salt. All red flags of bad nutritional habits. His own father had died from a massive heart attack at the age of sixty-three.

All those worries, however, were countered by Daddy's good habits. He didn't smoke or drink. He ran, played tennis, and since retirement, had a relatively stress-free life. Mel Johnson was the happiest man I had ever met. (He had, after all, told me, "You know, Miss, I'm already happy. Once you're there, you can't get any happier.")

So the idea that Daddy had suffered a stroke, however slight, upset the balance of my life. This feeling—this slight nagging at the beginning of every day—this unwelcome and unexpected awareness of change had given new dimension to my morning awakenings.

Would Daddy be well enough to cook meals for the hungry every Thursday night at church, a volunteer task he enjoyed? Would he still gallantly drive the "Miss Daisies," the older church women, to their weekly outings? Would he ever run another mini-Marathon or travel with Mother to some exotic locale?

Health crises like this one made me more sympathetic to others, more understanding and compassionate when someone said, "My dad is ill," or "My mom just had a stroke." Daddy's stroke also made me acutely aware of the passing of time. It moved me from a theoretical musing on the inevitable demise of *all* men to a very real and personal fear that one particular man would never be the same.

Multitudes of people like Daddy make excellent comebacks. Multitudes of people who love each other must be plagued with this uncertainty, this recognition of change, this unnerving sensation of worry.

No one is exempt from problems, and the ever-churning cycle of life makes the demise of parents an inevitability. Mine is not a unique or particularly frightening experience, just a sobering one that made it hard to get out of bed on those blustery winter days.

WHEN DADDY CAME HOME FROM THE HOSPITAL AFTER HIS stroke, I was there, some of my fear about his recovery dissipating. Thrilled to escape the confines of hospital beds and closed rooms, Daddy couldn't wait to return home again—home to his flowers, his keepsakes, his artwork, his family memories, his house, his life.

As we sat in the sterile, gray-painted room waiting for the wheelchair that would transport him to the car, Daddy turned to me.

"Miss," he said quietly. "Do you know the old movie called *Snake Pit?* It's about a woman who gets out of a mental institution."

"Nope, Daddy. I don't think I've ever seen that one." I patted his arm.

"Well, I feel just as happy to go home as she did in that old movie. I am getting to go home when I thought I might never be there again."

In a shaky, hoarse tenor voice, right there in that hospital room, Daddy sang the song he remembered from the movie. "I'm coming home. Coming home…" as tears rolled down his cheeks.

32

DADDY'S ANGEL

"I could not have made it this far had there not been angels along the way."
—Della Reese

"Now you can laugh all you want," Daddy/Gramps said, "but it's true. I know I have a guardian angel, and I know he talks to me sometimes."

Katie and Cassie could hardly control their giggles, and Allison, the friend who was eating dinner with us, clearly didn't know whether Gramps was crazy, joking, or dead serious.

I had no doubt that my dad was sincere. He didn't care whether we believed him or not. He had no reason to invent this story.

The stroke he'd had in January of 1997 had changed him, but he was still considered one of the "lucky" ones because his speech wasn't affected much, his shaky gait was stabilized with the use of a cane, and he could laugh and communicate just like he always did. The only lasting symptoms were numbness in his face, loss of balance, and the strange and total lack of desire for his much-loved coffee.

"It doesn't even smell good anymore," Gramps would moan.

Looking directly at the smirking girls, he went on with his story. "Yesterday, I was dumping some grass in the compost bin that we share with our neighbors. You know me. I'm a little rickety now, and I lost my balance and fell." Gramps held his hands up in a *c'est la vie* manner and shrugged. "That night, my glasses were missing. I looked everywhere. I couldn't see to read the paper, so I just decided I'd go to bed and worry about it in the morning."

The girls listened intently, even though they looked at their plates so they didn't have to show how interested they really were.

"Then early yesterday morning, in the gray before dawn, I heard something." Gramps, always a storyteller, paused dramatically.

"In a deep, but soft voice, an angel said to me, 'They're in the compost bin.'"

Katie's eyebrows raised. Cassie glanced at her friend before all three girls turned to Gramps' animated face.

"Well, as soon as the sun came up I got dressed and went over to the neighbor's. He even came out to help me look for my glasses. We dug through the whole bin, tossing clippings from one side to the other. We couldn't even get to the bottom of the bin because we would have had to stand on our heads, and Bud just had hip surgery. The only other thing we could do was to dump everything out on the ground, and I didn't want to do that."

"I was tired and dirty, ready to write off the angelic advice I'd heard in the early dawn as a product of my weird imagination, when that exact same voice quietly urged, "MELFORD, LOOK AGAIN."

"As soon as I looked down, I saw them. Sure enough, my glasses were right underneath a clump of grass where I'd been resting my leg." Both hands raised to swear to the truth of his tale, Daddy smiled and continued his story for the wide-eyed girls.

"I went back home and plopped down on the back deck, watching my yard, and you may not believe it, but I heard that voice again. My angel whispered, 'Mel, you ought to try a cup of coffee.' So I did. I went inside, made a cup, and that summer morning, for the first time since my stroke, I truly enjoyed the taste and smell of my coffee.

"But that's not the neatest part," Gramps declared to me as the young girls around us leaned forward in their chairs to hear the rest of the story.

"This morning when your mother and I left to come up to Danville, we pulled the car out of the driveway. In the dry cement where the car had sheltered the drive from the misting rain, was a perfect rendering of an angel with his wings outspread."

Katie, Cassie, and their friend, Allison, all blinked, clearly wavering between belief, astonishment, and cynicism. As for me, I trusted every word Daddy said that day. I fervently wanted his simple faith to rub off on everyone in that room. I wanted all of us to believe in angels and in the ability to find good omens in a scary, complicated world. I wanted each person in that room to have Daddy's passionate belief that God sends angels to watch over us. I wanted my girls to believe Gramps because in the long run, there are many less likely things than hearing the voice of your guardian angel and seeing his picture painted in your driveway.

33

A YOUNG GARDENER

*"My garden along the side of the house is doing well. I have 8
tomato plants, plus one potted deck tomato plant which has two
tomatoes set on. I have carrots, beets, parsley, peppers, onions,
celery, and zucchinis. Alongside the house is a good place as they
get 6-8 hours of sun a day. Even I might grow a little with those
conditions. Maybe I'll try and lay out there some. Just look for a
tall Gramps/Daddy."*
—Letter to Missi, May 23, 1999

The old man leans on his shovel, gazing down at the
beds in my garden, tottering slightly in the blustery air
as he bends down to break up a lump of soil.

He was shaking his head and muttering, "What good soil!
Such rich dirt. This is going to be the prettiest bean patch
you've ever seen."

A temporary obsession with planting seeds in my garden
had taken hold that frigid spring day. "Nothing," he declares,
"could keep me from doing what I want to do today. Not the

cold, not the damp, not the wind. The only thing that could stop me is if the wind blew me right off the face of the planet."

The stout figure trudges up and down, carefully defining rows with his hoe, dropping seeds with his gnarled fingers, sculpting cold, wet dirt hills with his old practiced hands. The more he plants, the faster he moves. Years fall off of him as he plays in the mud and metaphorically dances in the dirt.

Daddy. That very old man in the misty morning shimmers in an aura of age. His once raven-black hair shines silver, but the waves and cowlicks are exactly the same as in his Navy picture taken when he was seventeen. The slender physique and wiry build seen in old black and white photos have morphed into a round barrel-shape. His eyes still sparkle, only now that sparkle is magnified with the optical aid of bifocals.

Thomas Jefferson once said, "Though I be an old man, I am a young gardener." Like Jefferson, the elderly Mel Johnson is a very young gardener with his eternal optimism that life will come again. Spring will bring green no matter how cold the winter. Seeds will come to flower regardless of the barren ground in February. Watching Daddy, I understand that the man walking unsteadily around dirt rows and mulch piles is doing what he loves, planting seeds to remind me of our time together, of the bounty he wishes for me, of the love he pats into the ground to put forth roots, grow, and multiply.

Watching Daddy and spending time with him in the garden is wonderful, but it is also like being smacked in the face with a shovel. I suddenly recognize how old he is and how short our time together might be.

Not long ago, the father of one of my friends died suddenly. He was a vigorous, intelligent, kind and amiable man, and his sudden death shocked and devastated my friend. During her grieving process she often lamented, "I just wish I had had a few more days. I wish there had been more time." When another friend lost her ninety-six-year-old mother, a woman who had been unwell for years, she echoed the same thought, tearfully musing, "If I had only had a few more days."

And so I observe Daddy puttering around in my garden, having fun just spending time with me. Just so you don't think we're saints or have some kind of perfect relationship, I will admit that I get annoyed with his single-minded obsession with planting without paying attention to the detailed garden drawings and meticulous plans I had laid out for him at breakfast. He wildly beds my squash with the pumpkins. Then throwing caution (and seeds) to the winds, he madly sows decorative gourds amidst the tomatoes. (What kind of chaos might result from such flagrant botanical cohabitation?)

My irritation with Daddy's carefree planting style is brief because I enjoy his company so much. In my heart, I know that the time will come when I, too, will say, "I wish I had had more time."

There is never enough time with someone you truly love.

34

A DROP IN THE OCEAN

"Thursday, I drive the Daisies to Community Awards Day. Last
Wednesday, I took a van load on a "Brown Bag Adventure" to my
friend's place in Harrison County. We had a beautiful day, lunch
on the porch overlooking the river, and singing from some old
hymnals. Everyone seemed to have a good time. Then we stopped at
Polly Freeze" for ice cream on the way home. We don't move so well
anymore, but we still know how to enjoy the simple things of life."
—Letter to Missi, June 22, 1993

What happens when equal parts generosity and kindness are mixed with abundant joy?

A person is born who loves doing good deeds.

Daddy had that special mix of humanitarian traits.

"His best quality was his concern for others," Father Pete remembered. "Your Dad was such a generous person. Not when we were growing up, but in later years. You'd accidentally find out that he'd driven somebody to the doctor, or taken flowers, or something like that. He just kind of offhand mentioned it. And I attribute that to his Mother…The nice thing about it is that he never came across as being religious when you were talking to him. Then these many acts of kindness would come out."

Many acts of kindness, indeed. Too many to be counted.

Throughout his long, adult life, Daddy willingly, cheerfully, spontaneously did good deeds, not because he thought he could get into Heaven that way but because kindness flowed out of him like a spring from the ground, natural and unbidden. His favorite activity was "Driving the Miss Daisies," a group of elderly widowed or single church women who went on outings once a month. The group was originally named something else, but Daddy, always fond of word-play, called them the "Miss Daisies" after the Jessica Tandy/Morgan Freeman, 1990 movie. The name stuck. Piling into a church van, Daddy, the chauffeur, escorted them to shows, shopping trips, and innovative excursions. He truly enjoyed joking with them, talking with them, and taking part in all the outings.

Reading his letters from past years, I am reminded of both his service and his joy in giving it.

I have been taking the "Miss Daisy's" on a trip about once a month. I am driving them this Thursday to lunch and then to the IMAX in Louisville. Next month we are going to Derby Dinner Playhouse to see "Meet me in St. Louis." They always enjoy getting out and are appreciative. (March 17, 1992)

I am keeping very busy and loving it. I worked at church yesterday on the air conditioner. Saturday, we re-did the altar rail; stripped and refinished it. It looks much better. Last Wednesday I drove the "Daisies" to Derby Dinner and we saw "The King and I." (May 19, 1992)

Maybe it was Daddy's proclivity for eating that made his

other favorite good deed the Thursday night, "Feeding the Hungry" at church, a job he enjoyed doing for years. Not just about the cooking, it was also about menu-planning and procuring the supplies.

> *Molly has gone in to the office and I have to go do my Tuesday chores. I pick up bakery goods at Kroger's, which they give us for the needy poor, and then I deliver the altar flowers to the shut-ins. I get as much from that as they do.* (October 19, 1999)
>
> *I cooked for the hungry yesterday. We only had 55. For some reason, our count has been down. Maybe it's my cooking! Anyway, it's a lot of work, but it is such a good crew that you can't help but enjoy it.* (April 28, 2000)
>
> *I cooked for the hungry yesterday. I am co-cooking captain, and it is a lot of work. Yesterday, I thought I was going to be very short of help, but several new people showed up and it worked out. I guess the Lord sent them!* (late May or early June 2000)

Ringing the Salvation Army bell at Christmas. Parking cars for Harvest Homecoming. Singing in the Choir. Whatever he could do to help, he did.

"I signed up today for Ring the Bell for the Salvation Army through our church. (4 times—1 hour each.) I do this every year and rather enjoy it as I see a lot of people." (November 14, 2001)

Enjoy standing out in winter weather, flapping your bell-weighted arm to a group of total strangers? Only those blessed with a preponderance of the "joy-gene" like Daddy could find it pleasurable.

Dozens and dozens of people benefitted from his acts of simple kindness, much of it not connected to church. Putting together impromptu bouquets and delivering them, just for the heck of it, to people he knew. Fresh produce, beets, peppers, onions, tomatoes, lettuce, and kale would be bundled into a bag and handed over with a grin. (Who doesn't want a huge bundle of kale?) If someone needed a ride to the airport or the doctor, Daddy would volunteer, always willing to befriend anyone who needed help.

"Today, I'm taking my handicapped friend, Dan, fishing out at Virg's. He, Virg, doesn't know it yet, and I have to call him. I met Dan at the Y. He has had MS since birth and is confined to a wheelchair. He works out regularly at the Y, and like a lot of handicapped people is well-built above the waist from having to use his upper body so much. He has a good mind, and we enjoy each other's company. He is 34, likes to read, and music. He is also very proud of his independence. He just moved to Louisville a year or so ago into an apartment designed for handicapped people and struggles to make it on his own."

Daddy was a "giver," and that trait didn't just apply to charitable acts. His tangible gifts were wonderful, too, because they were chosen because he *knew* they would be right for you. He gave me my favorite possession, a carving of a woman's head—something he found in an antique shop and thought I should have.

The bust of the beautiful lady tilts her head slightly to the right, lost in thought. Exotic features. Delicate lines. Tawny woodgrain. Another woman. Another time. Another culture. Connected somehow to me. Daddy smiles at me every time I look at her.

December 1, 1999

Missi,

Last week when I went with my friends to Joe Ley's, I saw this hand-carved figure on the 3rd floor, stuck way back on an old bookcase. I thought, "Missi would like that." I did, too.

Every day I thought I should have bought her. Yesterday I went

*back, and luckily, amid all of the other thousands of things, she
was still waiting for me.*

*I wish I could find something as right for Melanie and Michele
as I thought this was for you.*

Merry Christmas, Tiger, (a nice Tiger.) I love you!

Daddy believed he was getting more than he gave, but he
didn't realize the enormity of his simple good deeds. He
could not know the accumulated mass of joy he brought to
others throughout his lifetime. Small things given freely.

Mother Teresa once said, "We know only too well that
what we are doing is nothing more than a drop in the ocean.
But if the drop were not there, the ocean would be missing
something."

Without Daddy, the ocean no longer roars.

35

DADDY AND THE BLIND CAVE FISH

"Pete was down Friday. We were going to play tennis, but it rained,
so I took him to a yard sale, and then we had breakfast. He and Bill
Jamison are coming down again this Friday and Saturday. We
might go to Farmington, a historical place sort of like Locust
Grove. They also like to drive along the scenic Ohio River."
—Letter to Missi, August 22, 2001

W hen too many stories start with "I don't expect you
   to believe me," there's a tendency *not* to believe.
Now, way too late, I've validated the one story that was the
hardest to accept.

I thought I knew everything, just like any other adult
child of an aging parent. At a certain point, parents pass the
stage of reliability, and so I listened to his stories with a grain
of salt. I was sure, even at this late stage of his life, Daddy was
making things up to add excitement to his tale. Or maybe the
seventy years that had passed since then had colored his
memory. My rational adult side had, after all, won the battle

against the childlike gullibility that believed every word Daddy uttered when I was a kid.

But one of Daddy's tale tales was verified by two expert witnesses.

I should have known just by his facial expressions that there was something to this one. Even into his late eighties, Daddy's face lit up with wonder when he told his story. Recounting the events of that day, he became more animated, he talked faster, and his hands gestured emphatically.

"Pete and Bill and I were hiking across the fields around New Albany, and I think a couple of other guys were with us, but I don't remember. I know Pete and Bill were. We used to jump on the train outside of town, travel through a large tunnel, and then keep riding for another ten or fifteen miles. Then we'd hop off and hike around there. That's where we first came across the sinkhole. It was really deep. Since Bill was the lightest of us, we told him we'd lower him down."

Daddy's hands moved around as he talked, trying to get us to understand the excitement of the find.

"Well, the hole was *really* deep, about ten feet square, straight down. Here we are, a bunch of guys, wrapping a rope around Jamison and lowering him in."

"Bill wasn't ten feet down before he started yelling. He was bouncing against the side of the walls. All he could say was, 'My jacket! My jacket!' We had to heave him back up, complaining all the time, before we decided to come back later with a longer rope and explore more thoroughly."

Daddy was on a roll now, telling his story to the audience gathered around the old, cramped, kitchen table.

"We weren't a mile from the sinkhole when we saw the opening. A skinny black hole just under a limestone over-hang. When we got to it, we could just barely squeeze in."

Daddy could always laugh at himself. "I was a lot thinner

seventy years ago!" he said as his hands patted both sides of his belly. "And yes, I COULD get in!"

Apparently, in addition to his other gifts, Daddy was also a mind-reader since several of us were thinking what a change age had brought to Daddy's physique. He knew he had our attention, and kept on going.

"You won't believe this! After we squeezed through the opening, we were in a cavern big enough for us all to stand in. Lo and behold, there was a stream running right through the middle."

I couldn't figure out the whole idea of squeezing into a sinkhole, and I wasn't sure how far the drop was. The whole adventure just didn't come clear in my mind, but it wasn't my story, so I just kept listening to Daddy's excited voice.

"But what I'll never forget was the blind fish. Can you imagine? BLIND FISH! I didn't even know they still existed. I thought they were prehistoric! And here they were in a cave in Southern Indiana that we had discovered."

Daddy kept waving his hands, his face alight.

"I was standing right in front of real, blind fish in this undiscovered cave. Here we were, a bunch of guys in this unmarked, hidden hole in the ground, big enough to have a river running through it, watching these funny, almost-transparent little creatures with no eyes. Fish that had never ever seen the light of day! I'll never forget that."

The sense of wonder in his voice. The amazement on his face. That was what we saw and will never forget.

Until he died, Daddy repeated that story. He listed as one of the biggest regrets of his life not going back, finding that cave again, and notifying someone about its existence. He was sure that he and his friends had been the first people ever to discover those teeny transparent fish. Forget Indiana Jones. In his mind, he was Indiana Johnson.

Daddy, who had been part of the out-of-doors since he

was born, who had traveled all over the world, and who had delivered a baby with his own hands, ranked those blind cave fish as the most amazing thing he'd ever seen.

His loved ones always doubted. We tried not to roll our eyes at what sounded like exaggeration, and we marked the cave-talk up to the wistful wanderlust of an eighteen-year-old country boy telling a tale in his old age.

Our shame came later.

Imagine my chagrin when Father Pete verified that Daddy was telling the absolute truth.

"Now, Melissa, what your Dad told you *was* true! Your dad, Bill and I, and a couple of others actually found a sink-hole *and* a cave. What your father didn't tell you is that the sinkhole we found was thirty feet deep. He may not have been worried about lowering Bill into the abyss, but the rest of us were. Well, actually, we were more worried about hauling him back up than we were about dropping him in. It's a lot harder than it looks, pulling dead weight against gravity on a single rope. But you know your dad. He didn't worry about much. He was pretty carefree."

Father Pete's old eyes sparkled. "And yes, the cave was real. Just as your dad had described. It had a stream running through it with tiny transparent fish. And your father was definitely *not* exaggerating about Bill yelling about his jacket!"

Even a non-anecdotal source confirmed Daddy's tale. Richard Powell, of the Indiana Geological Survey, said Daddy would have been walking through an area described as having "numerous sinkholes mostly along hillsides and low ridges adjacent to stream valleys. A few of the sinkholes have openings into cavern passages, most of which are small and short, but a few are large enough to walk in and some have a stream in the cave. Blind Cavefish has been seen in some of the caves in the past..."

Believe it or not (to echo Daddy's words), just a few years ago, a new species of cavefish was catalogued. Named "Hoosier Cavefish", they are the first new species of cavefish to be discovered in the U.S. in forty years, existing only in the area of southern Indiana where my dad claims to have seen them first, while walking through the hills in the early 1940s.

So heartfelt apologies to you, Daddy, and the hidden caves, giant sinkholes, and blind cavefish of southern Indiana. Now I can say with absolute certainty, that dead men tale no tales, and that Father, (and Father Pete,) really do know best.

36

BLACKBERRY ESCAPADE

"I am enjoying summer as usual. I picked blackberries Monday,
Wednesday, and Friday last week. Carmen picked with me
Wednesday, and Friday, Wendy. I have made a blackberry cream
pie, blackberry orange jam, blackberry cobbler, and frozen the rest."
—Letter to Missi, June 18, 1999

L ate in their life, but when they were still able to travel,
Mother and Daddy would come visit us in Illinois and
stay a few days. Sometimes it was for the birthday of a
grandchild, sometimes for a special event, and sometimes,
just for a visit. Mother enjoyed sitting and having great
conversation, something I learned from her and appreciated
about her. Even as she was dying, she wanted to converse
about what was going on in the world, movies, books, and
fashion.

Daddy, on the other hand, would be "champing at the bit,"
(a Daddy colloquialism), ready to go outside. He wanted to
do something: smell the air, talk to the plants, identify the

trees, survey the landscape. One weekend visit, he informed us of his intention to take a long walk through the open meadows of our property. Since this is what Daddy did wherever he went, no one blinked an eye.

About an hour later, I gasped when I looked out the front windows.

Just coming over the hill of the meadow staggered a man festooned in purple and white, looking for all the world like a giant, variegated eggplant.

My dad was absolutely purple. Everywhere. Face, arms, crotch, legs.

"Guess what, you guys? The blackberries are in!" he yelled as soon as he walked in the door.

At this point, Daddy was eighty. Since his stroke, he shuffled a bit when he walked and was content just to plod along in his own routine. He existed in his own world, and his world was the natural one, a place that provided a bounty of fresh fruit if you just looked for it.

Mother was livid at seeing her husband so thoroughly smeared with blackberry jam. Being angry for my unemotional mother meant that she grimaced and sighed. Loudly. And she got nasally. "Meeeeellllllllllll.....,"she would say, stretching out his name for a full two seconds through gritted teeth.

Anyone who ever knew my Dad understood that to him, clothes were only something you had to wear, and if they were stained or torn while enjoying life, it really didn't matter. Mother, however, was Daddy's self-appointed wardrobe manager, always thinking about what would be appropriate for Daddy to wear. To be fair, she had just bought him this new summer outfit. A crisp new pair of beige slacks and a fresh, soft white knit polo shirt, both of which were now totally tie-dyed with berry juice. His pants had purple bursts of blackberry smush all over, and thorns had pulled fibers in both shirt and slacks, leaving hair-like strands trailing in all different directions. No detergent on earth would be able to erase these stains.

It would be impossible to replicate the state of Daddy's dress that day. Even if I tried, I could not have gotten so splattered with purple juice. What do you have to do to wear a layer of blackberry preserves? How could Daddy have so blithely done this to himself?

The Jolly Green Giant himself could not hold a candle to Daddy, the Playful Purple Picker.

My husband Bill and I call this the Blackberry Escapade, one episode that emphasized the opposite side of the spectrum my parents inhabited. We often wondered how two people with such different personalities and approaches to life could ever co-exist. My parents were nothing alike in how much they cared about appearance. Mother, dressed impeccably and incapable of "dressing down", was horrified by how Daddy looked that day. Daddy, as usual, was oblivious, happy about his outdoor adventure, emitting a violet glow as he raved about the blackberry cobbler I would make for his dinner.

37

ALTERNATIVE REALITY

"He made them, the vicars of his love."
—Saint Ambrose

One Christmas Eve, when we were gathered around that crowded table set up in the living room, Father Pete said to Daddy, "You know, Mel, sometimes I envy you and your beautiful family." Last Christmas, nearly twenty years from that first remark, his Christmas card to me read, "I miss you and your family—especially at Christmas."

In my vision, the land of "might-have-been" reigns. I imagine Father Pete wearing, not black, but a sweater the color of the ocean. Two small boys run after him as they walk along the rocky, drift-woody banks of the river. His gentle voice says to the boys, "Now when your Uncle Mel and I were your age..." I can almost smell the damp earth and hear the questions of the boys.

A sweet, smiling, brown-haired woman is in the kitchen with Mother, helping prepare Christmas Eve dinner for the two best friends and their families. "Uncle Pete" appears in a plaid sports shirt and dark jeans. In the big mirror behind the piano, I see all of the Petersons standing around the piano bench singing carols with us as Daddy's hands dance up and down the keyboard.

My vision of this sweet and wonderful man as a father fades quickly, and reality sets in.

My mind tries to balance the scales. Is it better to have a life of service and nearness to God than to have a family and children to carry on your name? Wouldn't a woman somewhere have been lucky to have found such a sweet-natured, intelligent, caring man as a husband? How strong does faith have to be to cause you to forsake what most people strive for?

Paul Peterson has been a priest for his entire adult life, spending more than seventy years in the service of his church. In the course of his lifetime, he has prayed for thousands of people, but most especially for the families of his two closest boyhood friends. The Jamison kids and Johnson girls revere him as someone special, utterly dear to us. He gives blessings at our weddings and our baptisms. He is a part of family birthdays, holidays, and parties. He plays games with the next generation of children and asks questions about the jobs and hobbies of the adults, not because he is obligated to, but because he is truly interested.

Mel, Bill, and Pete may have been like the Three Musketeers in high school, but over the years, life took them down different paths. Two married. One took the vow of celibacy and service by becoming a Jesuit priest and teacher. Their choices decreed that the Johnson girls and Jamison children will be the only "family" that Father Pete will ever have. I hope we're enough.

Paul Peterson's final retirement reception occurred at the Brebeuf Preparatory School in Indianapolis on April 27th,

2018. Father Pete is ninety and still celebrating mass. Those in attendance honored him, calling him the "Wisdom figure and heart of Brebeuf, a model of faithfulness, humility, and a heart open to the direction of God."

Father Pete himself said, "Looking back over my life—or anyone's life—you can see God's actions in so many things; how he has graced you and worked through you: the opportunities, and even humiliations, that come and how everything brings us into deeper relationship with God and therefore better able to bring His love to others."

38

THE PIE AND I

"We now have some Boysenberries in our ground. Virg had some back of his house and when he cut the grass, he would have cut them off, so I dug up about a dozen plants and took them back this afternoon.

They're very good. They're a cross between a strawberry and raspberry and grow on a vine like a raspberry. They grow a lot of them in California. I got about a dozen stalks. They cost $3.00 a dozen if you buy them from a nursery.

I'll grow 'em honey, if you'll learn how to make us some pies."
—Letter from Daddy to Mother, May 14, 1952 (Two months before they married)

"I wanted to tell you about the pie." Father Pete grinned and shook his head. My sisters and I had hosted a family party with Father Pete as the guest of honor. It was a celebration of his retirement at the age of ninety, the friendship he had with Daddy, and the impact he'd had on the lives of the extended Johnson family.

"Well, your Dad and I and Bill Jamison had gone out to lunch at that place in New Albany. You know, it's way out of town. A big farm-type place where they serve country-style food." Father Pete waved his hand, trying to whip the name out of his memory banks.

"The Overlook in Corydon," someone offered.

"No. That's not it." Father Pete rubbed his forehead, frustrated by his inability to remember the name.

"How about Lancaster's?" another voice suggested.

"No way! That was a buffet and hasn't been there for years," a different voice protested.

Father Pete tried again. "You know, it's way out there in the hills."

"Maybe, Huber's?"

"*Yes!* That was it!" Father Pete smiled with satisfaction, ready to continue his story.

"I think Bill Jamison was with us. We were into our seventies, and we'd all gotten together in New Albany for some reason. Maybe just to have a meal together. I don't remember the occasion."

Everyone around the table listened intently as Father Pete got ready to reveal a "Daddy" story we hadn't heard.

"After lunch, since we were all full of fried chicken and dumplings and a lot of other good food, we decided to chip in on one of their giant pieces of homemade pie and share a single dessert."

Father Pete was soft-spoken, but every word rang out clear. No one talked while Father Pete was talking, but I could see Kevin, Melanie's husband, across the table smiling like he'd just been awarded a Nobel Prize. He was guessing the ending to any story involving both Mel and pie.

"Now whether it was because your Dad couldn't hear, or

because he was involved in conversation as he was eating, or whether he just couldn't help himself, I don't know. Bill took one bite and passed the plate to your Dad. Mel took one bite."

Father Pete went on. "Of course, I was patiently awaiting my turn. Even though we were full, that fresh peach pie with a scoop of vanilla ice cream did look awful good. Bill had raved about how light and flaky the crust was, so I was anticipating that final touch of sweetness to finish our meal."

"I watched as Mel took one huge bite. Then another. Before I could even protest, he had shoveled in the last two bites and the plate was clean, slicked over by his fork. Every last trace of peaches and crumbs of crust were gone."

Laughter erupted, but it was tinged with disbelief. How could Daddy be so oblivious to his friend? How could he not remember the deal to split the pie? How could he eat every dessert in his path with his severe diabetes? We who loved Mel/Daddy/Gramps could visualize the scene perfectly. Daddy was passionate about pie.

"That's one plate that never got passed to me. I never got even one bite of pie." All these years later, Father Pete still shook his head in astonishment at his friend's bad manners and gluttonous behavior. But he was smiling, laughing at his friend instead of being angry.

Lucky for Daddy, Father Pete is a gentle soul, a sweet man, and a priest who understands the forgiveness of sins.

39

THE LORD'S TIMETABLE

"First, I got up and had two cups of coffee sitting on my deck. Then I worked in the garden. I'll give you some tomatoes when they get ripe. I'm going to have dozens."

"Then I jogged across the bridge, took lunch to a sick friend. After our lunch, I'm going to church for a quick meeting, and then I'm coming home and taking a nap. What a wonderful day!"

The friend, observing Daddy's obvious joie-de-vivre, "exuberant enjoyment of life," shook his head, chuckling.

"Mel, I just hope you aren't disappointed when you get to Heaven!"
—Daddy's conversation with a friend over lunch

The three sweetest days of my life were the days when Daddy lay dying.

Ever since Daddy's stroke when he was seventy, he declared, "I'm ready to go!" We were glad he had survived his stroke, relatively unscathed, and were stupefied by his insistence that, "I wish the Lord would have taken me in those eight seconds I was 'gone.' I'm ready."

He must have seen our stunned looks, so he kept explaining his point of view.

"Think about it. I've had a great life. I've seen my children graduate, marry, and have children. I've seen my grandchildren graduate, marry, and have children. I've traveled the world. I've had a nice home, friends, and the love of a good woman. I couldn't ask for more, but I'm tired. I don't feel good. I'm just ready to go."

Eighteen years after his "bound-for-the-Hereafter" announcement, his family gathered around the hospital bed after Daddy's final, massive stroke. We were all fully aware of his "I'm-Ready-To-Meet-My-Maker" philosophy since he had repeated it to us individually at any opportunity. He had reiterated his belief to any assembled group of family on multiple occasions. For nearly two decades, his body had been in a constant state of decline, painful to witness.

There was no disputing that his chronic heart disease and rampant diabetes had lessened the quality of his life. No more jogging, swimming, gardening, or playing tennis. He couldn't drive, was unsteady on his feet, felt sick much of the time. His joyful days of volunteering were long past. Playing the piano, reading, and painting took too much energy. Instead, he sat on the couch, dozing, hour after hour. Waking briefly, Daddy would watch television with the volume so loud you could hear it when you pulled up the driveway. Doctor's appointments and funeral visitations were the major activities of his life. He no longer felt good enough to attend church on Sundays.

It seems so unfair that an active, vibrant man was so diminished by age and disease at the end of his life that he could do nothing but sleep. (When I get to Heaven, I am going to ask God—trying to control my anger—"Why couldn't You come up with a better exit strategy than aging into diminishment and decrepitude? God, *why?*")

Melanie and Kevin, Missi and Bill, Michele and Bob—all three daughters with the spouses that loved "Gramps" almost as much as they did—sat in that sterile hospital room with Mother throughout the next three days. One gray-toned room. One white bed straddled by a rolling tray table. One tiny nightstand holding an emesis basin with small bottles of mouthwash and shampoo. One push-button beige telephone. One window covered with blinds on the wall above a futon-like couch. One unremarkable, unmemorable room in a hospital that looked like thousands of others. One family's death watch, just like the millions other families have held throughout history.

In spite of the impending loss, Daddy's room never felt cold or antiseptic. Grandkids came and went, holding Gramps's hand and reminiscing about the special things he had done for them. Memories of camping trips and fishing tales. Wedding dances. Lessons learned. Each grandchild tried to be strong, but each one choked back emotion when remembering their experiences with Gramps. They said good-bye and stepped over the threshold of that little room into a world where Gramps was no longer telling stories, singing, or laughing.

Great-grandchildren were escorted in and out with their various parents. Bubbly little girls chattered to Gramps and presented him with pictures they'd crayoned. Boisterous little boys were subdued, yet courageous, as they approached Gramps' bed to pat his bruised, needle-poked, tube-infused, hands.

Four years old to eighty-three years old and every age in between, Gramps' family was with him, laughing and talking, conversing, crying, keeping vigil.

Daddy's mental function, we were assured by the doctors, was gone. Due to the massive stroke, he would never regain consciousness, but the pacemaker kept his heart pumping. No brain function existed. A mechanical device kept his big heart beating, fueling a tired body.

This is not what Daddy wanted.

Many siblings fight about what to do when a parent is dying. Often, a family is forever fragmented by their diverse beliefs about end-of-life treatments. One of the many blessings of my life is that when Daddy died, his wife, all three of his daughters, and all the extended family agreed on what course of action to take. We would do what Daddy wanted: let him go to be with the Good Lord.

It wasn't easy. It was painful. It was sad. It was right.

Luckily for us, Michele was a high-level attorney who worked in the healthcare field and for this very network of hospitals. She knew how to get through the proper channels.

Two of the doctors in charge of Daddy's care came into the hospital room shortly after Michele's appeal, and calmly, compassionately, asked Mother if she wanted the pacemaker turned off.

Mother could never make a decision on her own even though it was hers alone to make.

Chin quivering a tiny bit, voice tight, Mother looked at us. "Is this what we all want? Are you sure?" Every person in that room, daughters, sons-in-laws, grandkids, grandkid's spouses, and great-grandchildren, solemnly nodded, or choked out a whispered, "Yes." Our soft, cumulative voices made up a loud affirmative.

How often is a large family in complete agreement? Surely, the doctors were comforted and inspired by the love, devotion, and obvious attention to Daddy's wishes that hung in the hospital room air that winter night.

Daddy's pacemaker would be turned off, and he would

get his long-standing wish. His heart, without the aid of mechanical help, would just slow down and quit.

We waited.

The Lord keeps his own timetable. Mother rarely left the room, sitting quietly in a chair, stoic as always, resigned to the fact that Daddy would not be coming home this time. For the rest of us, real life, the life rushing forward outside of the hospital room where we cocooned, intervened with its own demands, and we came and went occasionally to answer phone calls or make arrangements to cover work. Most of the next three days we talked to "Mel," "Daddy," "Gramps." We remembered incidents...funny, sad, and poignant. Things Daddy had done for us. Ways he had taught us or advised us. Trips, quotes, and stories. Laughter floated out the room and down the corridors.

Sweetest of all, though, were the songs that swirled around his bedside, mists of music lifting him to Heaven. The hymns he liked to sing became our serenade. "This is my Father's world/I rest me in the thought/Of rocks and trees /Of skies and seas/His hands these wonders wrought." The Johnson girls and clan would sing the hymns that came to mind: "Blessed Assurance"; "Be Thou My Vision"; "Holy. Holy. Holy/Merciful and Mighty"; "The Old Rugged Cross"; "Amazing Grace." One of us would always know the words when someone else forgot, years of Methodist church services burned into the soundtracks of our brains.

Kevin, a kind, spiritual man, who had been Daddy's son-in-law for more than forty years, shared in a quiet voice, "I Can Only Imagine." We all listened or hummed along, lost in our own thoughts of what it will be like to get to Heaven, thinking of Daddy and imagining how happy he would be when he finally got there.

The most comfort for me came from singing Daddy's all-time favorite hymn:

"I Come to the garden alone,
  While the dew is still on the roses,
  And the voice I hear
  Falling on my ear
  The Son of God discloses.
  And he walks with me,
  and he talks with me,
  and he tells me, I am his own.
  And the joy we share as we tarry there
  None other has ever known."

Daddy loved that hymn because he had spent so much time planting and pruning, enjoying his roses, plucking the beauty to share with someone else, communing quietly with the Lord. I remembered all the times Daddy had spent in the garden with me. Ah, "the joy we share as we tarry there..." indeed.

While we were believers, we were not religious fanatics and certainly lived in the modern world. Popular music Daddy played on the piano by ear threaded their way through our tapestry of tunes. When the chorus to "Edelweiss" began, I was suddenly a seven-year-old, crooked-banged blonde, cocking my head at a jaunty angle. I wore a brown dress with shiny black buttons and stood in the living room, ready for a special event. The Johnson Family was going to see *The Sound of Music* with Julie Andrews. Even before we saw the movie, I was smitten. My parents (through the eyes of love) told me I looked like Julie Andrews, the star.

The year before, we had gone to see *My Fair Lady*. I don't remember what I was wearing that night, but I can still see Audrey Hepburn in a white nightgown, prancing around her bedroom belting out, "I Could Have Danced All Night." Even a six-year-old understands that kind of giddiness. Daddy's lasting memory of that movie though, must have been "On the Street Where you Live" because he often let the tune travel through his fingers to the keyboard. A couple of times throughout those days in the hospital, we drifted back to "The Street Where You Live."

But mostly, we sang the "moon" songs he was so fond of:

Shine on, shine on Harvest Moon,
For me and my gal,
I ain't had no loving'
Since January, February, June or July.
Snow time, ain't no time to sit –
Outdoors and spoon
So shine on, shine on, Harvest Moon.

At least three dozen renditions over several days were offered up, each of remembering the black-haired, smiling, youthful Daddy, singing with us at the piano:

Moon, moon, great big silvery moon
Won't you please shine down on me?
Moon, moon, great big silvery moon
Hidin' behind a tree....
There stands a man with a big shotgun,
Ready to shoot you if you start to run,
Oh, moon, moon, great big silvery moon.

None of us were fabulous vocalists, but we could all carry a tune. Melanie harmonized the alto part. Michele and I warbled soprano. Together, we sang the way he taught us to sing...with joy. For the fun of it. With gusto, like he had learned from his mother.

His daughters sang for him, the daddy who poured the music of life into our hearts.

Over the next two days and nights that followed his

stroke, his family thanked him for what he had done for us and told him it was time to go. We would be okay. We would see him again.

Kevin took the role of patriarch of the family since Daddy was no longer able to do it offering prayers on behalf of the whole, noisy, extended Johnson family. We held hands and prayed, not in some fervent fit of religion or in loud intonations of passion. We prayed in a hopeful imitation of Maw-Maw whose prayer prowess was legendary. We asked God, in sincere supplication, to take Daddy home.

Throughout his lifetime, Daddy had been physically active. All those sets of tennis and years of running and swimming had some effect. Even though the pacemaker had been off for two days, Daddy's big, loving heart was still going, erratic and slow, but still pumping. No amount of science can predict the precise moment the heart stops beating. No doctor can tell you when a tired old body will finally call it quits.

After three days of waiting and watching, we were exhausted, so we decided to take turns. Each daughter chose a night to stay with Daddy and Mother, freeing up the others to get some food and sleep.

Early Wednesday morning, the 15th of January 2015, I curled up in a chair next to Daddy's bed. Mother was sleeping on the couch. There was no sound except the high-pitched beeps and huffing sounds of machines. The monotonous noises put me to sleep, tired as I was from travel, worry, and hospital sitting. I drifted off to the mechanical sounds accompanying Daddy's breathing. It was an odd combo of noise and rhythm, the macabre wheezing of his chest accompanied by the bass of robotic beats. Guttural. Hard. Painful.

Daddy stopped breathing during those early morning hours of January 15th. Guilt slapped me awake when I realized that the sound of his breathing was gone. His chest no longer labored. He wasn't making deep, rattling noises anymore. Why was I dozing when I should have been holding his hand? How could I not have known he was at the very end? My eyes were closed and my heart was sleeping when I should have been singing him through the final gate of Heaven.

People have told me that patients often wait until no one is looking to "pass over," not wanting to cause pain or draw attention to the process. That would be so like Daddy, to die silently, going to the Great Beyond without even making me aware that he was leaving.

I thought of that night so very long ago when Daddy sat sobbing on the hearth, mourning the passing of his own mother. His words to me were: "It doesn't matter that she was ready to go, that I believe she's with God, or that no one can live forever. She was still the only Mother I'll ever have. For years, she said she was ready to meet her maker, that all-powerful, mighty God she talked about. I was wrong about not grieving. It hurts, and I'm so sad... No matter how old or senile, no matter how decrepit, how long they've suffered, it is still a loss for those who love them."

Daddy slipped away quietly because he understood the pain of good-bye.

IT COULD HAVE BEEN A BLIZZARD. IT MIGHT HAVE BEEN FRIGID. Rain, drizzle, or fog could have covered the earth that day in January. Instead, the weather was glorious for a winter day in southern Indiana: sunlit blue skies, no wind, and a temperature of fifty-seven degrees. We were sure that God was providing good weather for the "Welcome Home to Heaven" parade for Daddy.

"The best funeral I've ever been to," was a comment made not one time, but dozens of times as people walked through the receiving line.

"Well, we do put the 'fun' in funeral," Michele quipped.

Daddy's connection to Centenary Church had reaped gifts of friendship in the form of music. The church accompanist, a fabulous musician named Paige, switched between organ and piano and rendered the audience dumbstruck with the beauty of his playing. A world-renowned jazz musician, Jamey Aebersold, fellow New-Albanian, long-time member of Centenary, and good friend of Mel and Molly Johnson, played an alto saxophone rendition of "Amazing Grace" that would have brought Louie Armstrong himself to his knees.

Mother and Daddy had both gone to Indiana University and had volunteered tirelessly on committees and projects, "Hoosiers for Higher Education" being just one. They had sacrificed to send all three of their daughters to IU Bloomington. They had loved the sports teams, the campus, and the whole idea of lifelong learning. As a fitting tribute, we invited anyone who had attended IU (and there were many) to stand and sing the Alma Mater under the direction of Lynn Lewis. Long-time family friend, former choir director of Clarksville High School who had positively impacted the lives of all three of us Johnson girls, a former Centenary choir director, and the President of the Indiana University Alumni Association, our beloved Lynn Lewis led the song.

The ensuing melody was beautiful and right ringing through the walls of that hundred-and-fifty-year-old sanctuary:

"Come and join in song together,
  Shout with might and main,
  Our beloved Alma Mater,

> *Sound her praise again.*
> *Glorianna, frangipanna*
> *'ere to her be true.*
> *She's the pride of Indiana*
> *Hail to old I.U.!"*

The weather, music, and singing were just the warm-up acts. Michele, consummate attorney and orator, delivered a eulogy that was just like her: stunning, witty, eloquent. People laughed out loud at the funny stories of Daddy eating cat food, skinny-dipping on trips, telling tall tales. They smiled at the memories of the flowers he had brought them or the cobblers he had made for them. Friends and family recognized the six decades of his service to the church and community and his sixty-two-year marriage to Mother.

Father Pete, eighty-seven himself, said a sweet prayer of blessing for his best friend of more than seventy years, a feat which must have been difficult, even for a man of God.

"It's a good thing when the sanctuary explodes in laughter and when music pours forth at the end of someone's life," the minister told the three Johnson girls as we stood in the front row right before we acknowledged more than a hundred people who filed passed us to give condolences.

Shortly after the procession from the church to the cemetery, we sat in a little chapel and listened to the last words of the minister, although I can't remember one iota of what was said. I do, however, remember with cutting clarity the words of the Navy officer as he marched down the aisle to Mother. I held her hand as those powerful words were uttered:

"On behalf of the President of the United States, the Chief of Naval Operations, and a grateful nation, please accept this flag as a symbol of our appreciation for your loved one's service to this Country. God bless you and this family, and God bless the United States of America."

The words held power. The moment was sanctified. Daddy, a seventeen-year-old enlistee who had served as a clerk for just two years at the end of the war, had been acknowledged for his small, clerical part in keeping the ideals of the United States alive.

A tear trickled down Mother's cheek, one of the few outward signs of emotion she had shown throughout the whole process of Daddy's death. She calmly let go of my hand so that she could accept the folded flag. Clasping her slender fingers together, blue-veins pulsing, Mother rested her hands in reverent silence on Daddy's flag. The solitary teardrop plopped down and left a dark spot on the blue field of stars.

Aa a bagpiper played "Amazing Grace," the long line of Johnson kin followed the coffin to the empty hole that would take Daddy into his beloved earth. Wife, daughters, sons-in-laws, grandchildren and spouses, and great grandchildren filed passed. Some plucked a final rose from the spray on his casket. Others touched the lid of the coffin. A few stopped in silent prayer, while many wiped their eyes and went on. Children, wide-eyed and quiet, held their parents' hands and turned their heads back to keep looking at "Gramps" as long as possible.

Relief and joy, sadness and happiness, life and death. A mixture of opposites blended into the heady, potent elixir of existence.

No one was untouched by the joy that Daddy brought into our world.

Melford Henry Johnson's physical body was buried in the family plot, next to Aunt Carol and Uncle Jim, Uncle Bill, Baw-Baw, and Nanny, who had been keeping company with her worms for years.

His soul, however, was set free.

40

THE BOYS OF SUMMER

"What I remember especially about your Dad was the overpowering love and friendship over the years. No matter what. No matter how far apart we were, no matter how many years we hadn't seen each other. I always felt that I could call on your Dad anytime. Anytime I got into town.

You know, when you look back on your life, you see so many gifts, so many blessings along with the trials. Your Dad was one of those blessings.

What I really want you to know is how much the love and friendship of your Dad meant. How lucky I was to have such a good friend."
—Interview with Father Pete, April 2018

"We did so many things together down there in New Albany. We had the hills. We had the river. Majestic, really. You know, we'd go hiking or canoeing. We'd camp overnight and come back home." Father Pete was, at the end of his life, willing to share so much about the youth he had shared with Daddy.

"You know, Melissa, your dad was kind of a carefree guy in some ways. He wouldn't be hindered by any obstacle. If you'd say, 'Well, this is difficult to do,' he'd just go ahead and do it. He didn't worry about it. In fact, he didn't worry about anything." The priest's smile never left his face.

"One time long ago," Father Pete told me, "he and Bill and I were hiking. Your dad decides he wants to show us some kind of rock formation. A ledge. A ledge that had a rock over the top of it like a cavern."

It was a strong visual picture. Three skinny, dark-haired teenagers ambling through the countryside of southern Indiana. The boys were just friends hanging out with each other, looking for adventure like kids used to do in an era before every waking moment was scheduled with activities, before everyone was glued to cell phones and computer screens.

"So your dad takes us to this special spot that he's found, somewhere back off the Ohio. It had rained. Mel's in front. Bill and I were following behind. He's walking along this barely-worn path on wet gravel on the side of this rocky outcropping. There's a big drop on the other side. And the path just disappears. There's no path there at all. Just a clod of dirt." Father Pete's hands gesture six inches apart to indicate the size of the space between the rock and the drop.

"Mel just goes…he just goes on through, not worried at all. Didn't even stop to consider his actions or pause to look at the scary drop or consider the lack of footing. He never thought that he could fall off the side or slip on the wet rock. He just wasn't worried. So we asked Mel, 'Are you sure it's safe? Are you sure we can get through?' Good ol' Mel was just trekking on ahead of us. He didn't even hear our hesitation.

"'There's no way I'm following him on that non-existent trail', Bill said to me. He just flat out refused to try. (He was a pretty smart guy.) So I went with Bill back down the way we had come, and we had to go down and around to the bottom."

This was a story I hadn't heard before.

"I don't even know if your Dad knew that we had turned around. He just kept right on going. If he did know, he just figured that we would meet up somewhere at the bottom. He wasn't worried. He never did. Unlike us. Bill and I just weren't as carefree as your dad," Father Pete concludes.

Was his tactful use of the word "carefree" a euphemism for "fearless," "reckless," or "stupid"?

Father Pete was always diplomatic.

"PETE AND I WERE ONLY ABOUT FOURTEEN OR FIFTEEN WHEN we got this idea to go down river to New Orleans," Daddy reminisced one evening when Father Pete was visiting and we all sat around the table. "It was a simpler time when you could hitchhike until someone picked up you, and then you'd ride in the back of a truck without worrying that you were going to be robbed or murdered."

The story came to us in bits and pieces over the years. Whenever we heard Daddy gearing up for the recitation of his "trip-to-New-Orleans-canoe-adventure-down-the Ohio-with-Pete," his girls would listen, silently evaluating the amount of truth in the telling. Knowing Daddy's propensity for exaggerating, it was easy to let cynicism slip in. Could this really be true? All of it? Could two teenage boys really just take off down the river on an unsupervised trip, for weeks at a time, with no itinerary or back-up plan? Could two kids cook and camp and fish on the uninhabited banks like Huck Finn and Tom Sawyer? Sounded like a tall tale to us.

When Father Pete confirmed Daddy's oft-told story, it went from being legend to being fact. A priest, after all, wouldn't lie, would he?

Daddy's eyes opened wider and his voice gained theatrical inflections as he continued his story. "Pete and I had saved all the money from our summer jobs for this adventure. We had a fourteen-foot canoe with a big sail." Spreading his arms as wide as they could go, Daddy demonstrated the immensity of the sail.

"Oh, yes, I remember, Mel. I'd worked on my mother's old sewing machine for days making that big canvas sail," Father Pete chimed in. "It was heavy, you know!"

Daddy raised an eyebrow, and pointed, "You know, Pete, fifty years later and I still have that sail. It's the best drop cloth I ever had!" Daddy grinned and jabbed his old friend lightly in the ribs with his elbow.

"More like sixty years later, Mel, and I'm glad to know that you valued all my hard work and craftsmanship enough to let it keep the paint off your floors." Pete clapped Daddy on the shoulder and chuckled alongside him.

"Remember the night when we were almost eaten by ants, Pete?" Daddy shuddered. "Hordes and hordes of these little red ants marching in crisscrossing lines that ran all over us. It was like they were double-timing just to get to us."

"Yeah. I think we finally gave up and found a hotel that night." Father Pete agreed, unconsciously flicking an imaginary bug off his arm.

"I was never so glad to have a bed with clean sheets!" Daddy groaned as he remembered thousands of tiny, itchy, red ants crawling over them.

Father Pete continued the telling. "I remember it was the last day of July in 1943 when we left New Albany. At that time of the summer the river was very low. No current at all, so we had to paddle most of the way. All muscle-power." The laugh-lines around Father Pete's eyes crinkled as he talked. "Remember when we went through the lock with the tugboat?"

"What I remember, Pete, is that it took us forever. Nine days just to get to Evansville." Daddy shook his head in remembered disbelief.

"Mel, I think it was eight days," Father Pete countered. "But you're right. It was slow going.

"So what happened? Did you finally make it to New Orleans?" I asked.

"Yes, we did, but not exactly like we planned." Daddy grinned. "We gave up, sold the canoe in Evansville, and hitchhiked to New Orleans.

Pete chuckled. "And selling it wasn't as easy as he makes it sound. We found a guy in Evansville who wanted to buy it, but he wasn't sure we really owned it. He thought we might have stolen it. Finally, we got him to believe us, and we sold it to him for fifteen dollars."

Melanie had always suspected that Daddy made up the part about them making it all the way down to New Orleans, but Father Pete confirms they really did. They did it by walking and hitchhiking, though, and not by paddling down-river in a canoe.

"New Orleans wasn't all that big of a deal. We hung around a few days watching the ships, listening to music, and walking around. Then we started hitchhiking home," Daddy said.

"So how long did it take you to get home?" Michele asked.

Father Pete gave a quick burst of laughter. "Not that long! By the time we started back, we were really, really, tired, so after a day or two of hitchhiking, we just went to the bus station and bought a ticket home. It was a lot faster!"

Ah ha! Daddy never admitted that they took the bus home. That fact didn't add to the aura of adventure he liked to create.

"But what about your parents? Didn't they worry?" I asked Father Pete.

"Well, my dad wasn't the kind to worry about me, and my mother was deceased. She died of a stroke when I was fourteen, a few days before her forty-second birthday."

A glimpse into the personal life of Father Pete was as seldom seen as a turtle stripping off its shell, but it made sense that after such a sudden and tragic loss of a mother, he would need friendship, companionship and a little escape into the wild with a fun-loving guy like Daddy.

That evening, the Johnson girls gained a newfound appreciation for the "New-Orleans-by-Canoe" story Daddy always told. Now we knew it was true. (Mostly.) In addition to Daddy's story being corroborated, we glimpsed the bond made between two skinny kids years before. Two "river rats" who, like Huck and Tom, set off downriver determined to have an adventure of their own. Two country boys who followed different paths, but whose friendship pulled them together time and time again in the fast and flowing current of life.

Father Pete and the Johnson Girls

41

THE VOICE IN MY MAILBOX

"p.s. I'm watching TV news about cloning. I'm putting in an order
for a dozen of me,
so watch out!"
—Letter to Missi, January 8, 1998

T he ordinary words of Daddy's frequent letters magically bring him back to me. His speech pattern, his humor, his delight in daily living permeate the paper. Daddy's writings, however, make him immortal. He jumps off the page in the words he wrote, as if he was still sitting next to me at the kitchen table, talking.

Take, for instance, this single paragraph from his letter of May 19, 1992:

"Just wanted you to know that last night I grilled pork chops out back on the grill you gave us. Thank you. I had wilted lettuce out of my garden and macaroni. I have also had kale and have given both kale and lettuce to friends. When I was a kid I wouldn't have

216

touched kale with a ten-foot pole, but now this old goat really likes it. In re-reading this paragraph, I'd like to clarify. I did not grow the macaroni in my garden. It won't grow in Indiana."

Then there's his silly, self-deprecating humor:

"Last week I went with Wendy and Chuck to Rough River. Chuck has a beautiful boat there. Then Thursday, played golf with Wendy, Evelyn, and another friend. I didn't realize it, but I almost got too much sun. It's a good thing I have a big nose because I have peeled off several layers. The weather has been perfect, and I am so fortunate to be mobile (even if I do stagger some at times.)"

The joie de vivre that pumps through his veins:

"Molly is still working hard, and I'm, as my shirt says, "Retired. My job is having a good time."

Always, always, his love of food:

"I couldn't sleep thinking how hungry I was. (Written at 4:30 a.m.) You'd be surprised how good bacon and eggs taste at 4:00 a.m.

Questions like, "How can anyone really be bored?" and "How lucky can one guy get?" pop up. Over and over again, he uses the word "Fortunate," usually in the context of an outing or trip he got to take. "Aren't we fortunate?" he so often asked.

Daddy wrote letters because he liked them.

"I've got this neat letter from one of my ancestors," he declared with pride. It tells about his capture by Indians and all sorts of gory details. Very interesting. And it was my family!"

As a young girl hanging on every word Daddy said, I fell

in love with letters, both in reading them and writing them. "Daddy's letter" is ensconced in Johnson family history. Written to his wife, Betsy, W.K. Jordan pens this missive during the war of 1812:

"I had to surrender myself to four damned yellow Indians," and he goes on to describe what they did to his captain, Billy Wells: *"...cut off his head and stuck it on a pole while the others took out his heart and divided it among the chiefs, and they ate it raw."*

Gruesome details, but compelling! Eventually my ancestor escaped and wrote Betsy again:

"I have two letters of yours and some of the soft hair of your head, some in plait around my neck. Tell me how you are, and how the children are, and for God's sake send Mountford to school...So I conclude with my best respects to you till death, or till I see you..."

W.K. Jordan never returned to Betsy, dying of pneumonia before he could.

Daddy's correspondence may not have been as historical as W.K. Jordan's, but it was filled with important things. Every week for the three years I was at Indiana University, Daddy faithfully sent a letter with a $5.00 bill in it. Mother and Daddy sacrificed much to send all three daughters to college, and even though I worked in the cafeteria to earn extra money, I was always cash-strapped. My parents didn't have a lot of income, and what they had, they used on us. Daddy had to scrimp to send me that money, but it wasn't just the five dollars that I anticipated. It was the encouragement, the positivity, and the sense of home that came in the note wrapped around the bill.

His money-letter was my "Coke" money, and it came

filled with encouragement and the breezy, happy news so like him.

> *"I had a complete physical last week. The Doctor gave me some non-cantankerous pills and said to call him in five years."* And *"News from my deck. The robins are busy feeding their babies. The sparrows, too, have a family in the birdhouse, and yesterday when I trimmed the holly, I saw a nest with eggs that the doves have built. I used my Christmas gift certificate that Molly gave me and bought geraniums for the front and two for the pots on the deck. I view the world from my deck."*

My tiny, long, metal key-box was so much happier filled with an envelope from Clarksville. A Coke machine stood at the entrance to the laundry room of my dorm, and after Daddy's letter came, I could run down the two flights of stairs to visit it. When that cold, glass bottle slid down and shot into my hands, condensation flew out in sparkles, tickling my fingers and tantalizing my taste buds. Most kids drank beer. Coke was my "get-high" ambrosia, and nothing pleased me more than the sound of the *PHFZZZ* when the bottle-cap popped off. Not many kids could say that their father knowingly supported their drinking habit.

Daddy's sweet generosity was lifelong. When I was divorced and taking Cassie with me to Hawaii on a group trip, an envelope came in the mail:

> *"Doing my bills this morning. Missi and Cassie, sending you a small amount for your trip. Sorry it isn't more, but maybe it will give you a little extra. I want you to have it. Have fun. Don't cash until Social Security Day, 6/3."*

He had little. He sent it to me.
My mailbox and I miss Daddy. The only thing that arrives

in the daily postal drop are throw-away advertising slicks, and I long for the permanence, the elegance, the tangibility of a letter. No more "joy-in-an-envelope" brightens my day. No more cheerful letters about gardens and friends and birds arrive addressed in Daddy's familiar script. I miss his voice.

Daddy's frequent sentiment echoes through my head. Aren't I "fortunate" to have the letters I have? Aren't I "fortunate" to have had this man for a father?

John Donne said, "More than kisses, sir, letters mingle souls."

He didn't tell us, however, that they also bring the dead back to life.

42

SWEET SORROW

"Be calm. God awaits you at the door."
—Gabriel Garcia Marquez, *Love in the Time of Cholera*

Father Pete, ninety-years-old, still gentle and smiling, arrived at Melanie and Kevin's house on Thanksgiving Day, hidden behind the huge bouquet of yellow roses and red orchids that he was carrying in his thin arms. His carefully penned card in the shaky scrawl of an old man read, "You don't know how much I miss Mel and Molly. Prayers and remembrance, always."

The extended Tolliver family and the extended Johnson family blend into a loud and loving group of more than fifty, gathered for the annual Thanksgiving festivities of dinner and subsequent "Turkey Bowl" touch football game. Daddy was gone, dead almost two years. And now Mother was gone, too, dead not quite three months.

Father Pete said to me, like he did every time we met, "Melissa. When are you going to get back to writing?

"Father Pete. I'm going to write about Daddy. And I need your help."

His smile overtook his whole face, pleased that Daddy, this friend and father that we both loved so fiercely, would be the subject of my first book.

While others played football, I tried to get a little clarification of his own story, but Father Pete was never forthcoming about the details of his life. Trying to get him to tell about his own life was like extracting solid material from a cloud. Still, I wanted to know, and thinking I would use something Daddy had already told me to get us started, I said, "Tell me about breaking your ankle parachuting into a tree during the war. And about the time you spent as a Japanese prisoner of war."

Father Pete burst out with a short, tenor "Ha!" followed by a wide grin and a head shake. Eyes gleaming, he told me, "Melissa, I broke my ankle in high school, not jumping from a plane, and I was *never* a Prisoner of War in Japan. I think your dad must have been confused."

"Well, he did have a tendency to exaggerate."

"Not really. Now Bill Jamison, *he* could exaggerate!"

"Okay, then. How *did* you break your ankle?"

"I was tumbling in gym class and tried something I had no idea how to do and broke my ankle. I heard it snap. And I did go to Japan, but I was drafted after the war and was sent over to Japan in the Army of the Occupation."

"Father Pete," I sighed. "Sometimes Daddy was just a little careless with the facts."

That chuckle. That wise smile. Father Pete shook his head gently. "Melissa, your dad was carefree. Not careless."

A differentiation I loved.

We continued our conversation, talking about our retirement, my children, and my grandchildren.

"Melissa, I want you to keep writing. I read many of your

columns, and I believe this is a talent you should be using. Your dad was always so proud of you." Father Pete took my hand into his thin, old one, patted it with his other hand while he spoke. "Your family has been such a blessing to me." He blinked a bit. His hands trembled just a little. "You don't know how much I miss your parents," he confided in that unassuming voice. "How lucky I was to be part of your lives. A true blessing."

I turned away, eyes blurred. I'd just witnessed a holy prayer of gratitude, uttered by a man I loved and would never forget.

FIVE MONTHS AFTER THANKSGIVING, FATHER PETE AND I SAT reminiscing about Daddy at lunch, more than two years after he had died. Together, we laughed at the boyhood memories and the stories Father Pete had either verified, modified, or denied. A recent eye surgery had not taken well, and he could no longer read. His two best friends had passed ahead of him, first Daddy, then Bill Jamison. More than ninety years old, Father Pete must have been feeling tired and lonely.

"I'm so glad we're doing this now, Melissa," he said, his smile sending light into the noisy cafeteria around us. "In a month or so, I'm moving myself to the nursing home for retired priests of our order."

I sat stunned, shocked. Never having given any thought to what happens to elderly priests, men without family, when they got too old or too ill to take care of themselves, I'd never considered that Father Pete might move away. Tears welled, and no matter how I tried to contain them, they rolled down my cheeks. This man, beloved to my family, the last link to my dad, was going far away, where he would die surrounded only by the brethren of his order, yet relative strangers to him. Who there would know about his southern Indiana roots? Who would know about the games he played to entertain the children of his friends? The Jesuit Brothers might share a devotion and rituals of the order, but would they love him like we do? Once he moved to the northern end of Michigan, none of the Johnson girls would be there to sing him to heaven or to hold his hand when he passed.

In the quiet of the car on an abnormally cold April day that spit snow, Father Pete once again took my hand in both of his before he quietly pronounced, as emphatic as any sermon, "What I really want you to know, Melissa, is how much love and friendship your father gave me and how much that meant to me. We had so many, *many* good times. I am so lucky to have had such a good friend."

His quiet voice was almost playful when he looked at me and continued. "I sometimes wonder what our bodies are going to be like in Heaven. I think of Jesus after the Resurrection when he says to his disciples, 'Look. You can come put your hands in my side.' But then they know he's different than he used to be. They don't quite recognize him, and I wonder what my friends are going to be like. I know we'll recognize each other, but we'll all be different. What are we all going to be? It's such a mystery."

Still smiling, Father Pete shared his hope.

"In fact, what I want to do in Heaven is get together with Bill and Mel and get rid of all the buildings in the United States. I want us to start on the East Coast and hike, ride horseback, canoe and camp, and go all the way to the West Coast, carefree and laughing, just like when we were young."

I want that too.

With all my heart.

The End

Keep reading to find your
The Magic of Ordinary Book Club Discussion Guide
Questions
by Melissa Gouty and Teresa Medeiros

Obituary

"Old as she was, she still missed her Daddy sometimes."
—Gloria Naylor

Melford Henry Johnson, 87, went Home to the Lord after a decade-long conversation declaring "I'm ready to go." Born in 1927, Mel lived his entire life in Southern Indiana, graduating from New Albany High School in 1945. Seventy years later, he still has close friendships from those high school days. His shorthand and typing abilities earned him a clerical position in the U.S. Navy which he served with pride from 1945 to 1947. He attended Indiana University and graduated with a Business degree in 1951. The next year, he married Molly Ann Wilson, his beloved bride of sixty-two plus years. Long careers at American Commercial Barge Lines and Stewarts Dry Goods showcased his hard-work ethic and humor, earning him the respect of many.

Work life was important, but in retirement, church life and volunteering in the community were paramount. He volunteered with Hoosiers for Higher Education and was a supporter of the Clarksville Historical Society. For more than sixty years, Mel was a faithful member of Centenary United Methodist Church giving joyfully of his time and talents in "Driving the Miss Daisies," cooking for the hungry, and singing in the choir.

Mel called himself a "River Rat," proud of swimming across the Ohio and embarking on a canoe trip from Louisville to New Orleans as a teenager. He loved the out-of-doors, gardening, cooking, (eating), music, swimming, running, canoeing, whitewater rafting, and tennis. But most of all, he loved his family. His legacy of love flows through the future in the families of their three loving daughters, the eight beloved grandchildren, and fourteen cherished great-grandchildren.

He was a good man, loved by many. Missed by all.

Daddy the River Rat

ABOUT THE AUTHOR

Melissa Gouty is an award-winning teacher, speaker, and entrepreneur who's been putting words together since she could hold a pen and making friends with book characters since she could read. A long-running newspaper columnist, copywriter, and blogger, Melissa created www. LiteratureLust.com, a website for readers, writers, and thinkers with an insatiable desire for the written word. Melissa recently turned her passion for writing into a full-time pursuit. Within nine months, she had given birth to her debut book, *The Magic of Ordinary*, a heart-warming, heart-wrenching memoir about growing up with a father who made life magical.

When she isn't reading, writing, or spending time inside her own head, "Missi" lives with her husband Bill, and their dog, Ella, in a Midwestern country home where they garden, entertain, and love life. If they're not there, they're traveling the country in their camper having adventures that would make her Daddy proud.

Visit Melissa's website http://www.melissagouty.com

Join Melissa on Facebook at
https://facebook.com/melissa.gouty.9

Join Melissa on Pinterest at https://www.
pinterest.com/MelissaGouty/

Literature Lust http://www.literaturelust.com

Sign up for Melissa's newsletter https://lp.
constantcontactpages.com/su/xXuG5Xd/LiteratureLust

The Magic of Ordinary Book Club Discussion Questions
by Melissa Gouty and Teresa Medeiros

1. What was your favorite scene in *The Magic of Ordinary*? What scene do you think you'll remember long after you put down the book?

2. Who was your favorite character?

3. The Johnson family had many experiences that ended up being "family legend"? Would you like to share one story from your family that ended up as "legend"?

4. Discuss Missi's feelings toward her older sister, Melanie. Do younger kids *always* adore their older siblings? Is her reaction to her sister's boyfriend typical?

5. Missi was lucky enough to have two grandmothers who influenced her childhood. Compare and contrast Maw-Maw with Nanny. Which woman seemed most realistic to you? What did you like best about each? Could you see any resemblance to your own grandmother(s) in these women?

6. Which traits of those grandmothers were passed to their offspring? How was "Daddy" like his mom? What do you see in "Mother" that might have been passed down from Nanny? How do you see those traits passed down and blended into the Mel and Molly Johnson's marriage?

7. Why is music so important to the Johnson family? How is that love of music reflected in the story? In the writing? Is music important to your family? Does it take away from the story if you don't know the melody or the song described?

Can you name one song that was a big influence in *your* family?

8. "Mother" (Molly) was not a warm and fuzzy person like "Daddy." Discuss her character and your reaction to her. What clues does the book give you about Missi's relationship with her mother?

9. To their middle daughter, Missi, Mel and Molly seem like an unlikely match. Do you believe that "opposites attract"? Do you know couples who seem mismatched, but aren't? What can you tell from the book about Mel and Molly's marriage? Do you think children are reliable interpreters of their parents' relationship? What did you believe about your own parents' relationship? Did you perceive them as well-matched or as a case of "opposites attracting"?

10. Every family faces the death of a loved one. Have your experiences mirrored or contrasted with the Johnson family's experience in the hospital when Melford was dying? Why do you think there was no squabbling or conflict within this large extended family when life or death decisions had to be made? Talk about your perception of the chapter, "The Lord's Timetable."

11. How would your family have reacted if presented with a situation like what happened to Mel Johnson in "Mysteries in an Electric Funeral Parlor"? Would the reaction be different today than it was in 1963?

12. There are two father figures in *The Magic of Ordinary*. Compare and contrast "Daddy" with "Father Pete." Discuss the role Father Pete plays in the book. How do you feel about him?

13. Each chapter begins with an epigraph—either a quote or a snippet from an original letter. How effective is that technique? Was there a particularly memorable epigraph? Pick a favorite epigraph and share it with the group, discussing why you liked it or how it related to the chapter.

14. How similar or dissimilar was your own childhood experience to Missi's/the author's? Is her experience vastly different from the experiences of children growing up today? If so, how? Will people who didn't grow up in the same era be able to relate to these experiences?

15. Melissa Gouty wrote human interest columns for eleven years and was often praised for writing about the "universal experiences" of life. Which experiences in the book would you consider to be "universal," in that while they're personal, they're also something that everyone experiences?

16. The author is a Midwestern girl. What elements of the book reflect a regional perspective? Will a child growing up in a city still "get" the book? Does "geography" outweigh "universality"?